THIS HOW TO DRAW

ANIMALS BOOK

for kids

BELONGS TO:

____

DEDICATION

This How To Draw Animals Sketchbook is dedicated to all the Animal lovers out there!

You are my inspiration for producing books and I'm honored to be a part of keeping all of your animal drawing information organized all in one easy to find spot.

HOW TO USE THIS ANIMAL DRAWING BOOK:

The purpose of this book is to keep all of your animals drawings all in one place. It will help keep you organized.

Learning to draw is with the grid copy method. It's a wonderful way to work on your animal observations and proportion skills while drawing. Comes with over 50 magical illustrations!

This animal drawing sketchbook grid copy method will allow you to accurately document every detail about learning to draw animals. It's a great way to chart your course through learning how to draw different animals.

Here are examples of the prompts for you to fill in and write about your experience in this book:

1. Monkey Drawing - For learning to draw different animals, including monkeys.

2. Your Turn - All your grid happy drawings. Use this space to practice drawing out animals.

Enjoy!

DEER

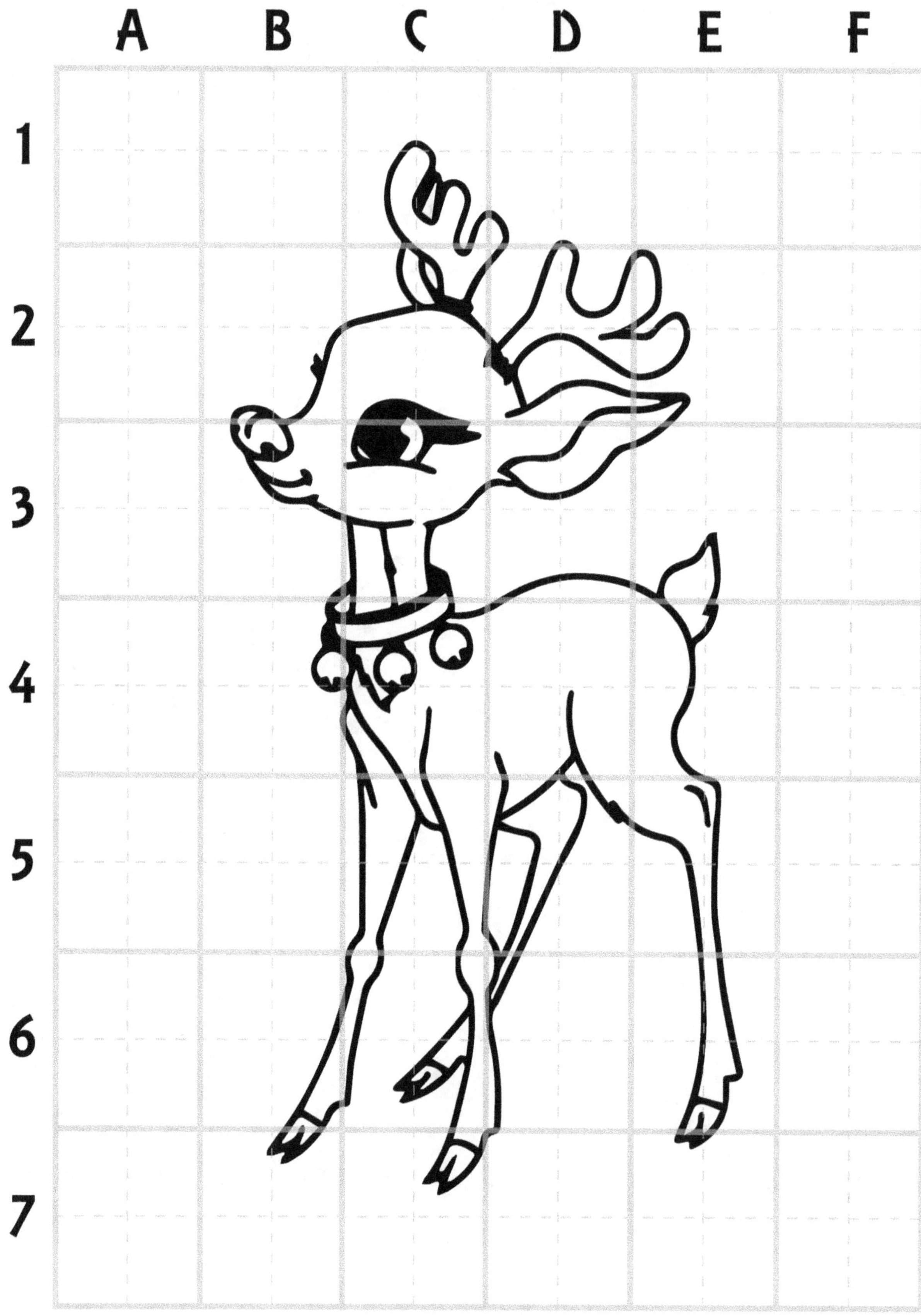

YOUR TURN!

	A	B	C	D	E	F
1						
2						
3						
4						
5						
6						
7						

LION

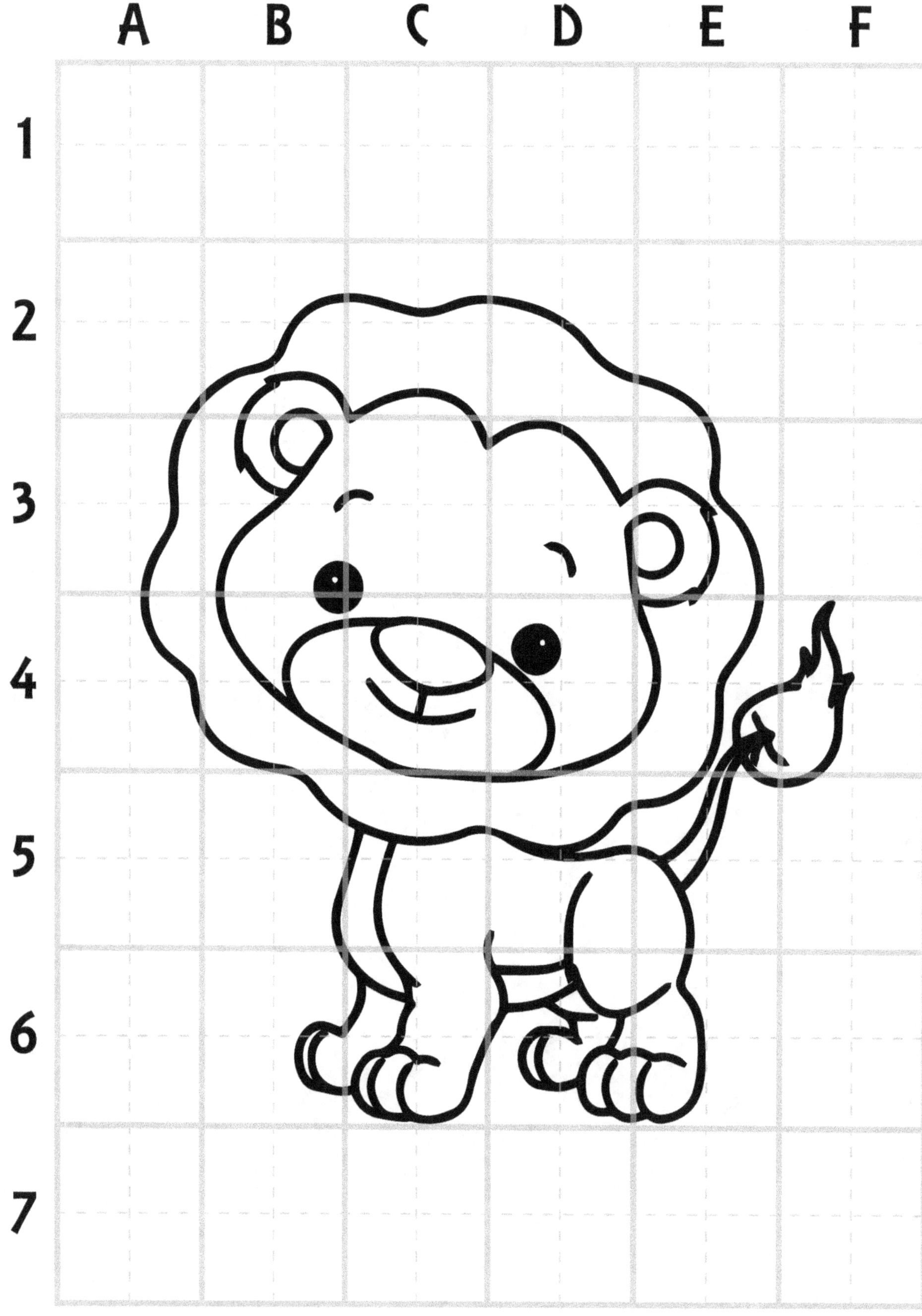

YOUR TURN!

	A	B	C	D	E	F
1						
2						
3						
4						
5						
6						
7						

GIRAFFE

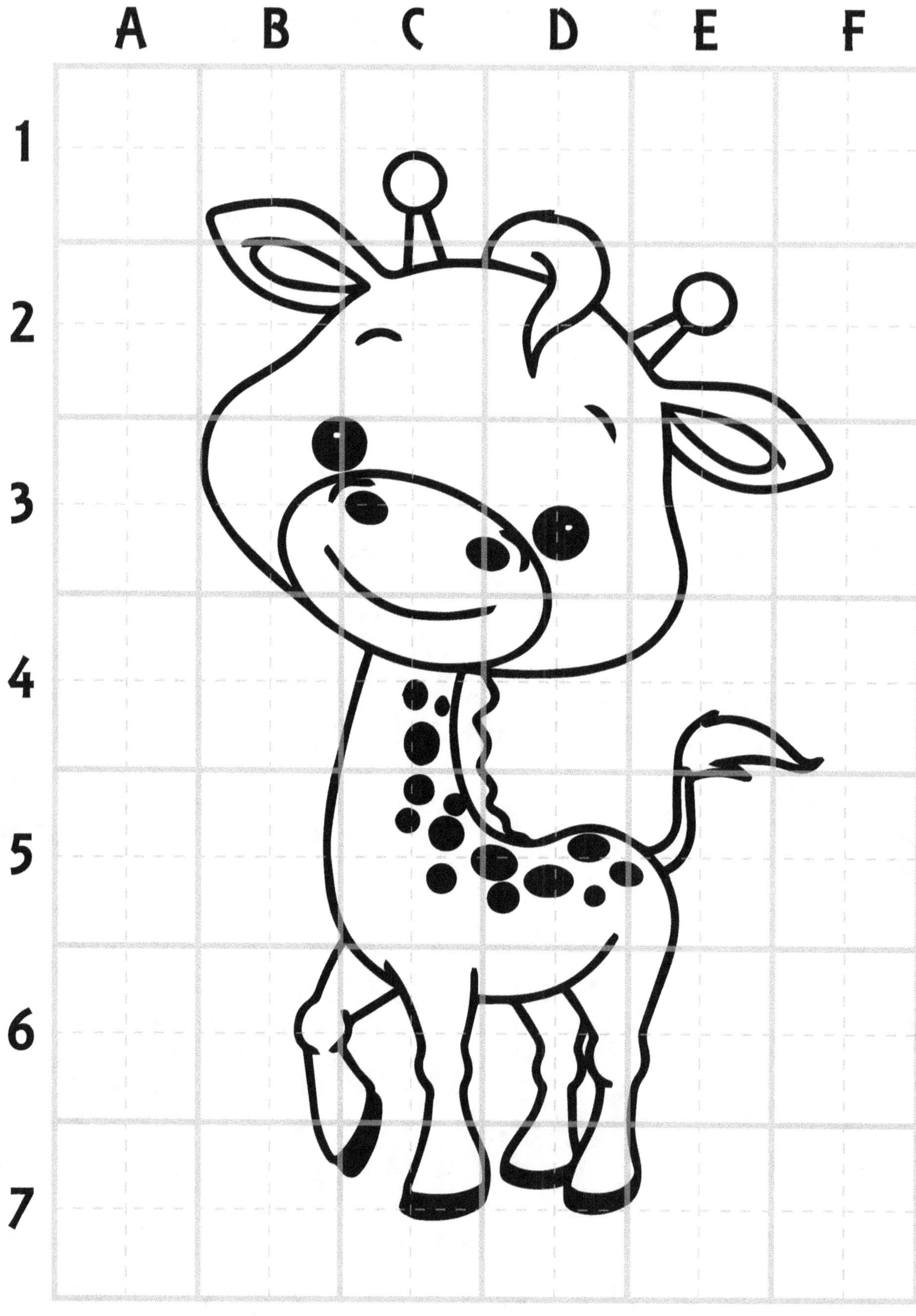

YOUR TURN!

	A	B	C	D	E	F
1						
2						
3						
4						
5						
6						
7						

KANGAROO

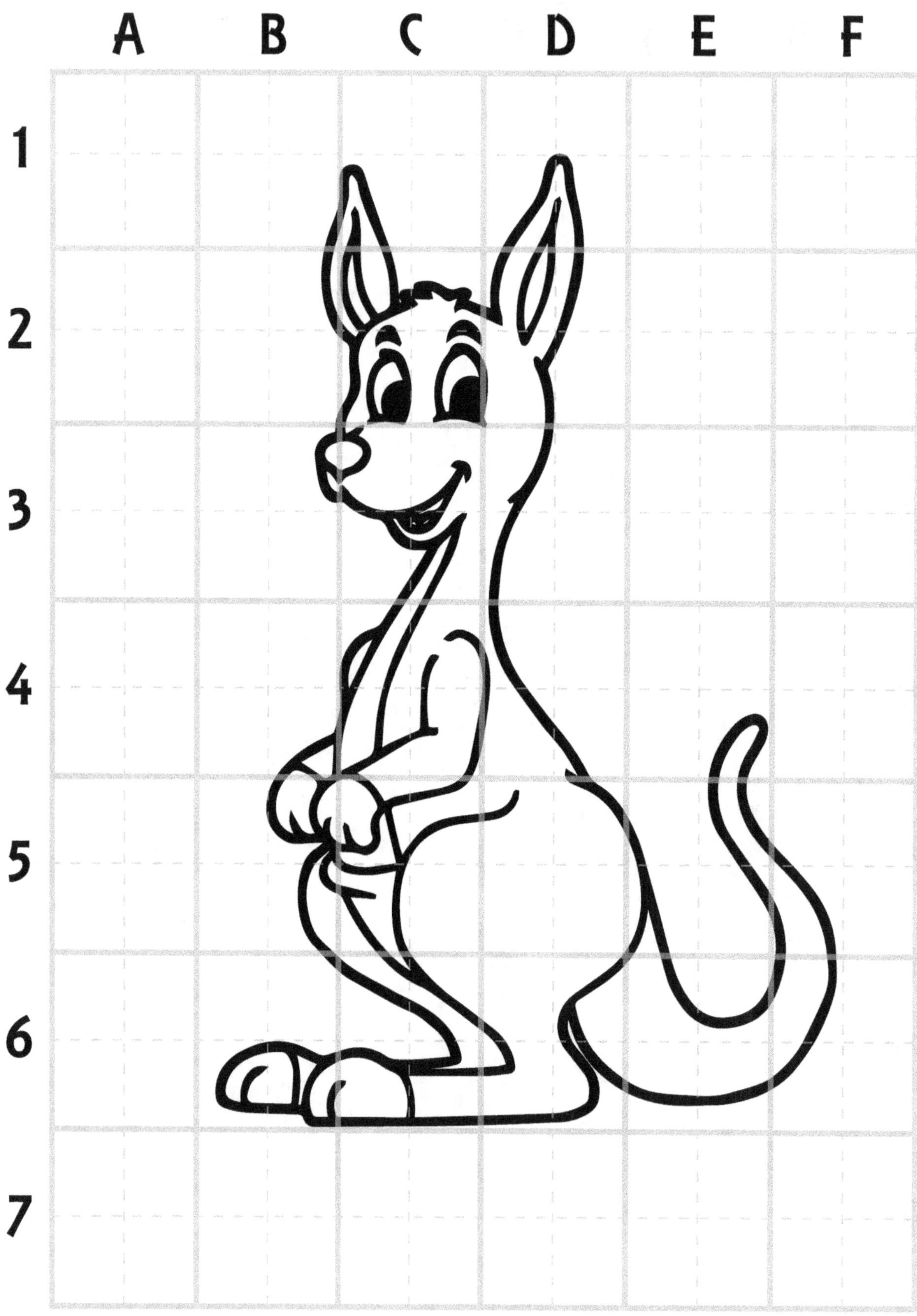

YOUR TURN!

	A	B	C	D	E	F
1						
2						
3						
4						
5						
6						
7						

ELEPHANT

A　B　C　D　E　F

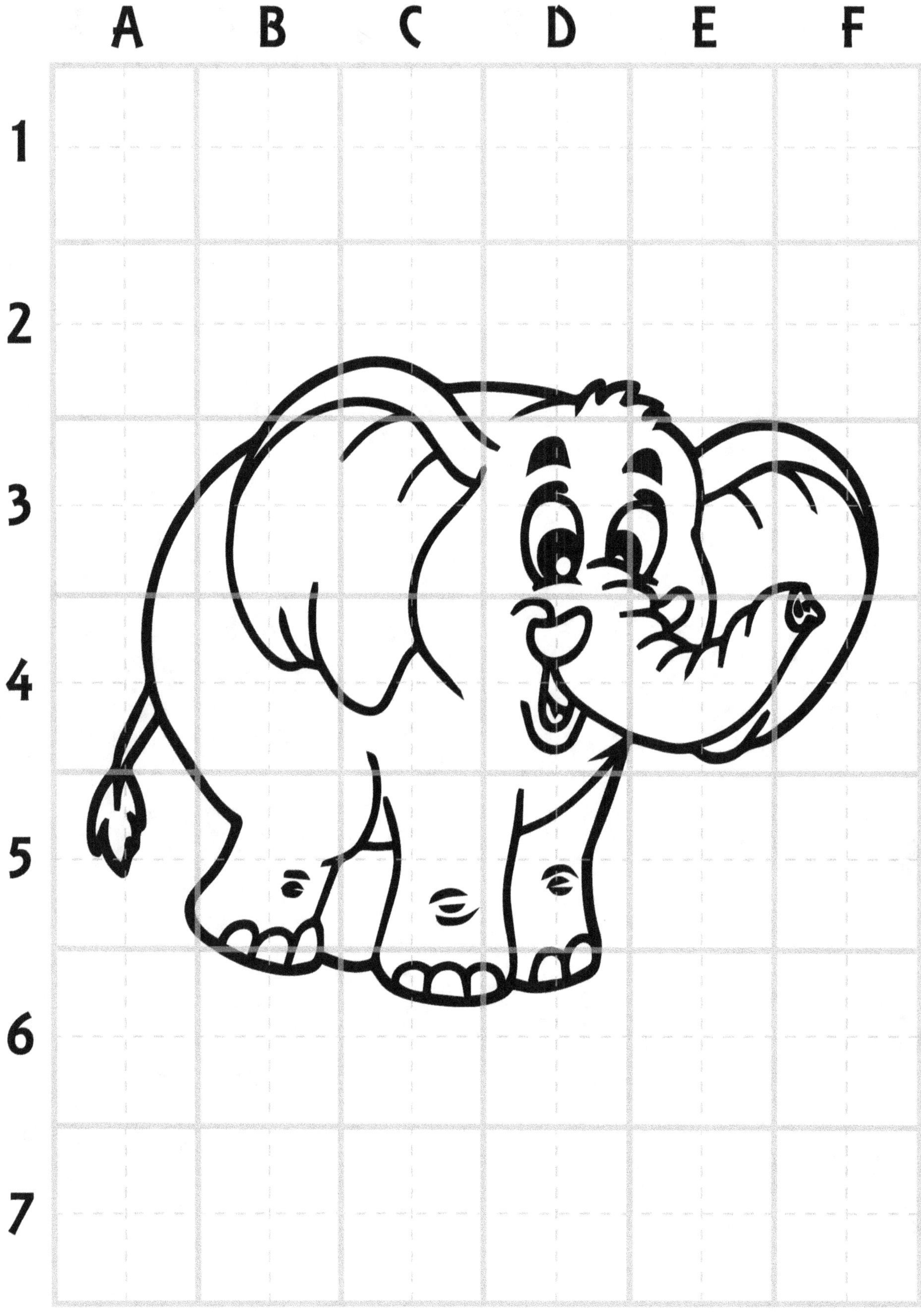

YOUR TURN!

	A	B	C	D	E	F
1						
2						
3						
4						
5						
6						
7						

PENGUIN

A B C D E F

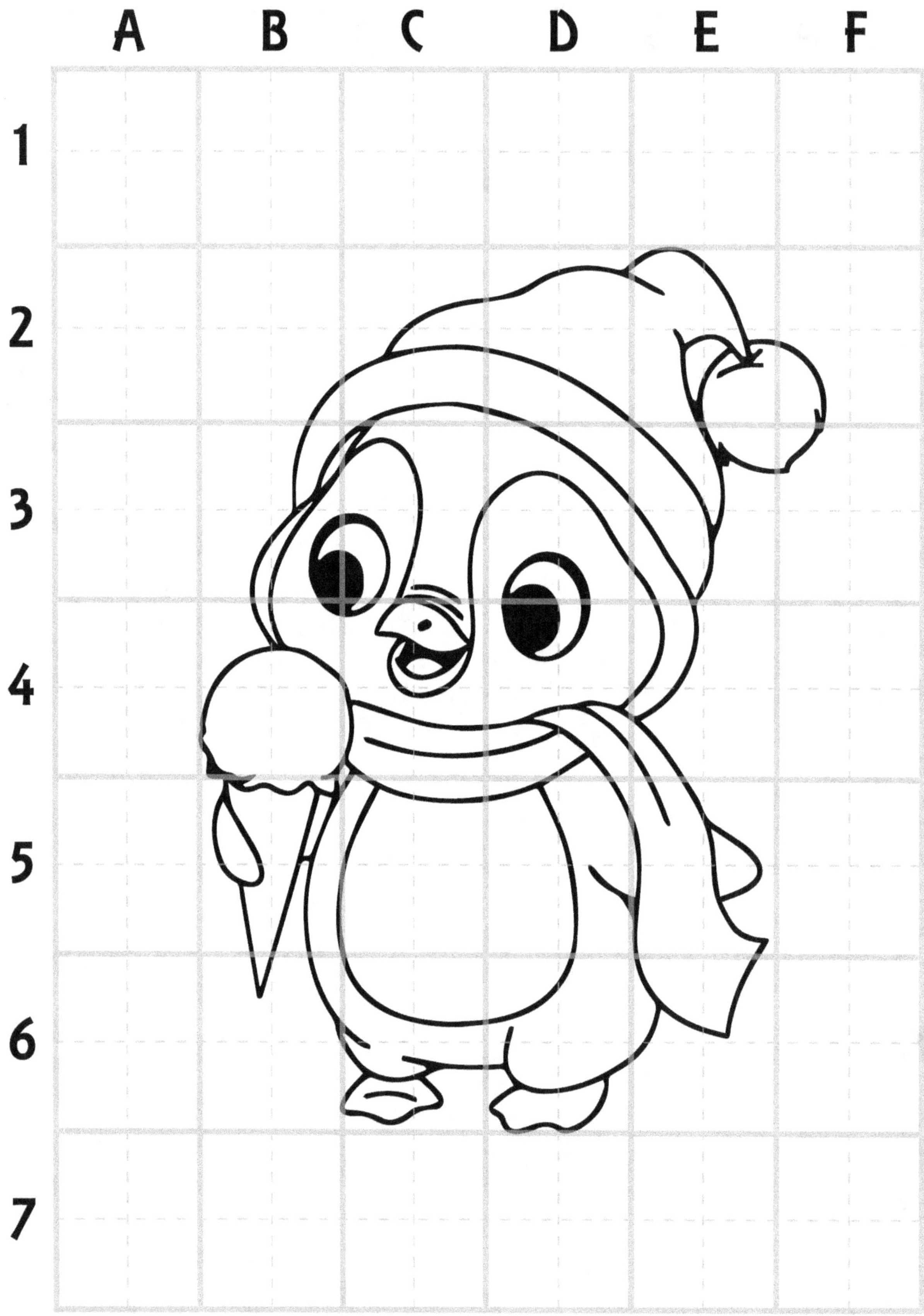

YOUR TURN!

	A	B	C	D	E	F
1						
2						
3						
4						
5						
6						
7						

MONKEY

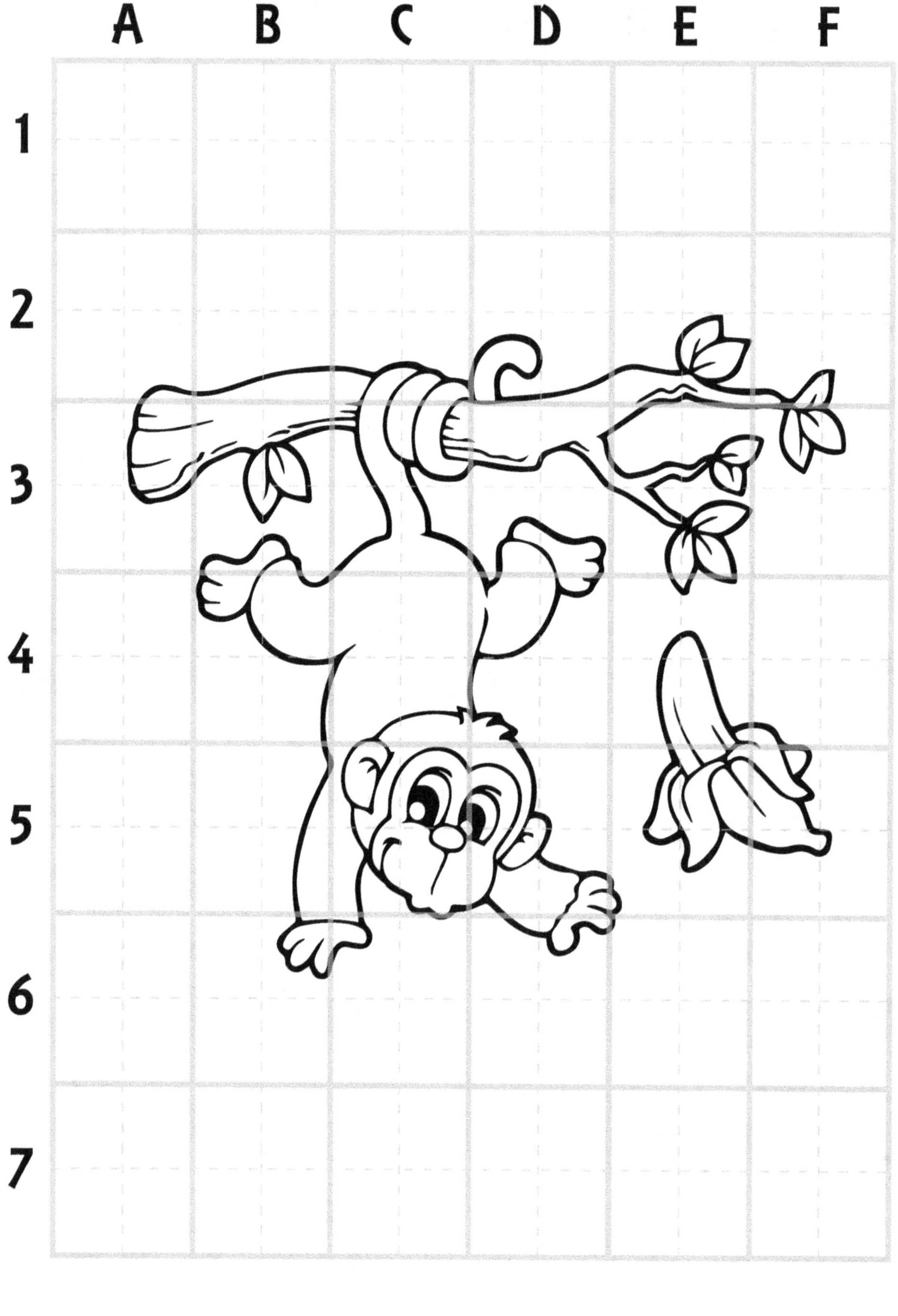

A   B   C   D   E   F

1
2
3
4
5
6
7

YOUR TURN!

	A	B	C	D	E	F
1						
2						
3						
4						
5						
6						
7						

CROCODILE

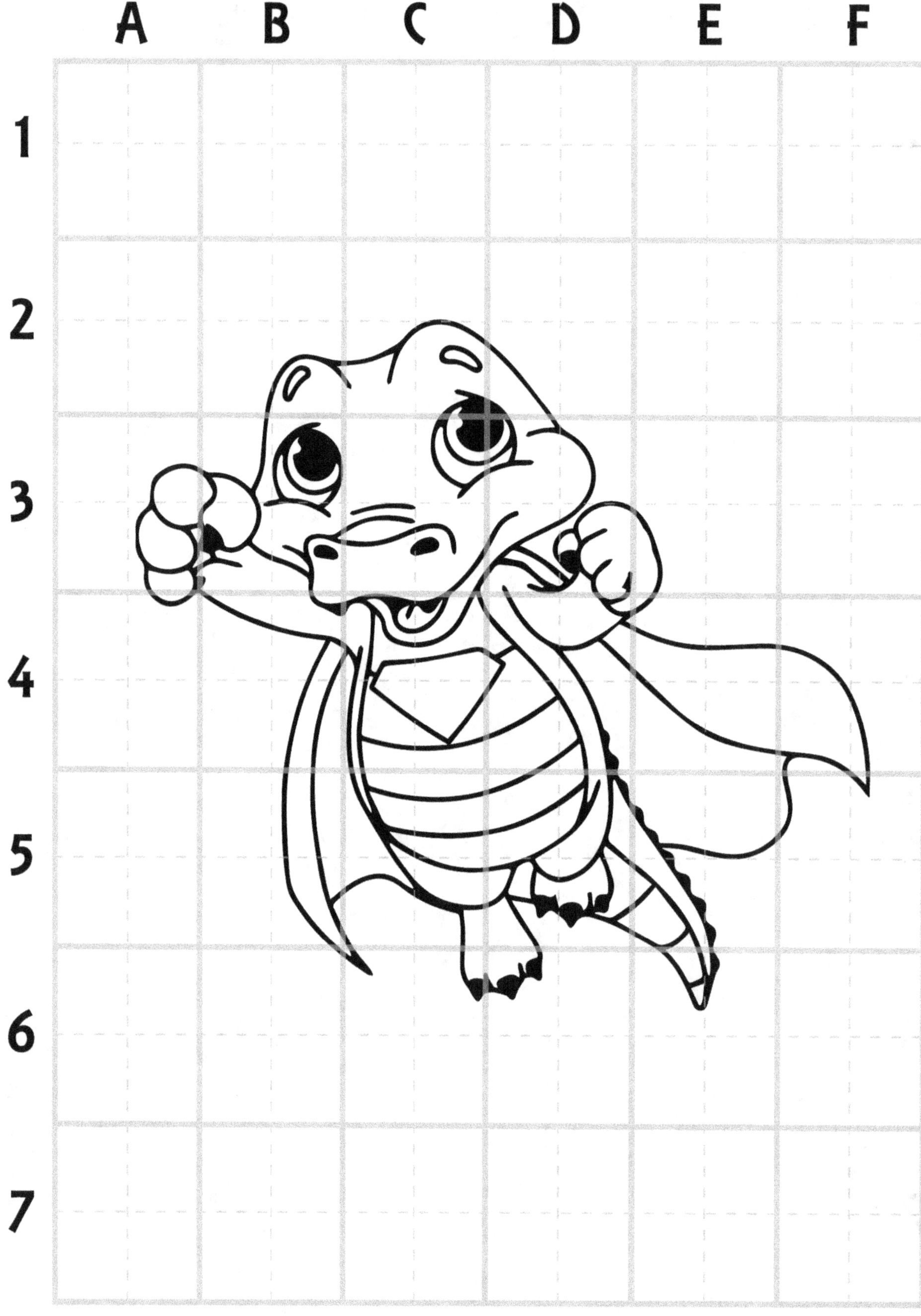

YOUR TURN!

	A	B	C	D	E	F
1						
2						
3						
4						
5						
6						
7						

BUNNY

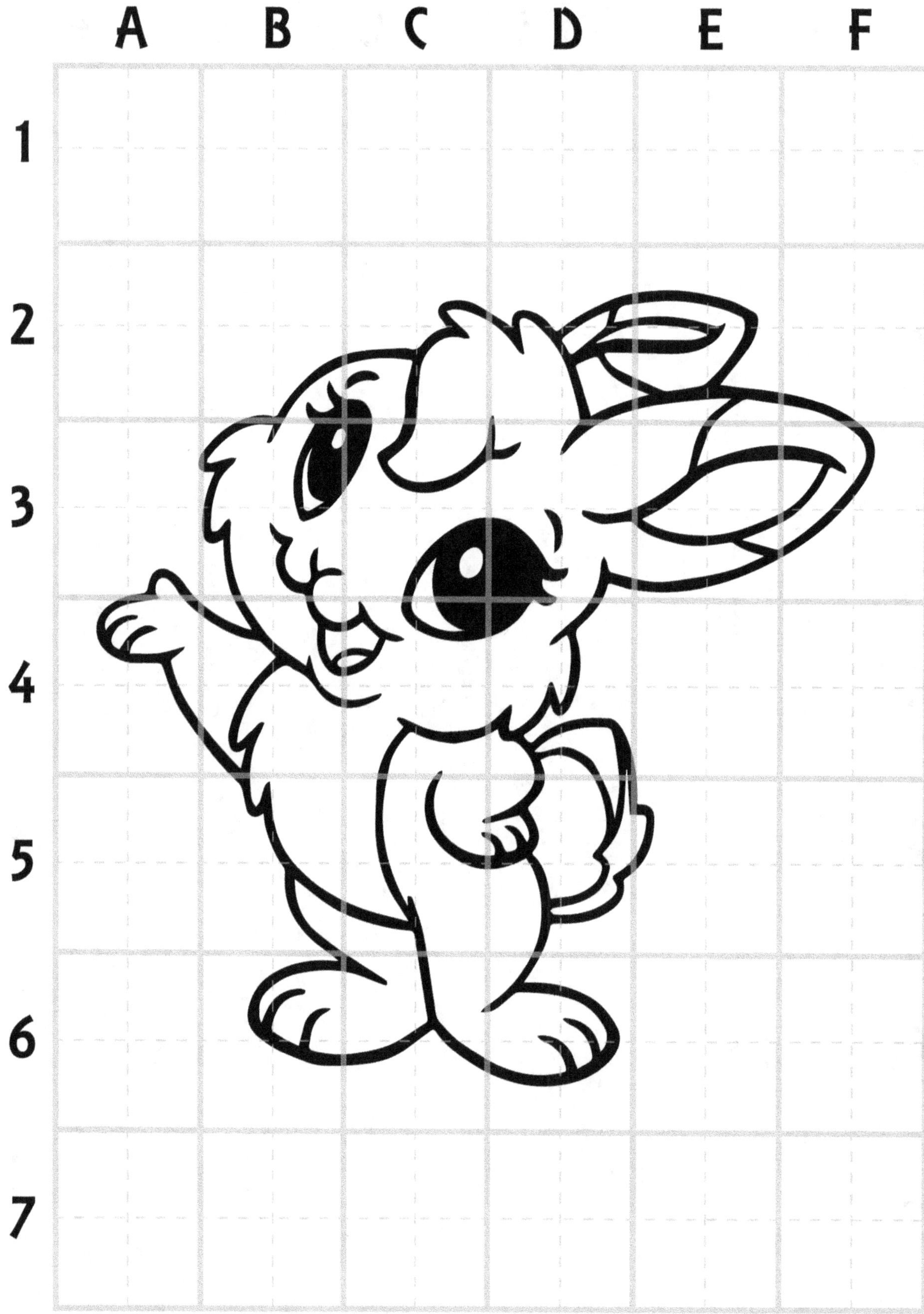

YOUR TURN!

	A	B	C	D	E	F
1						
2						
3						
4						
5						
6						
7						

SHEEP

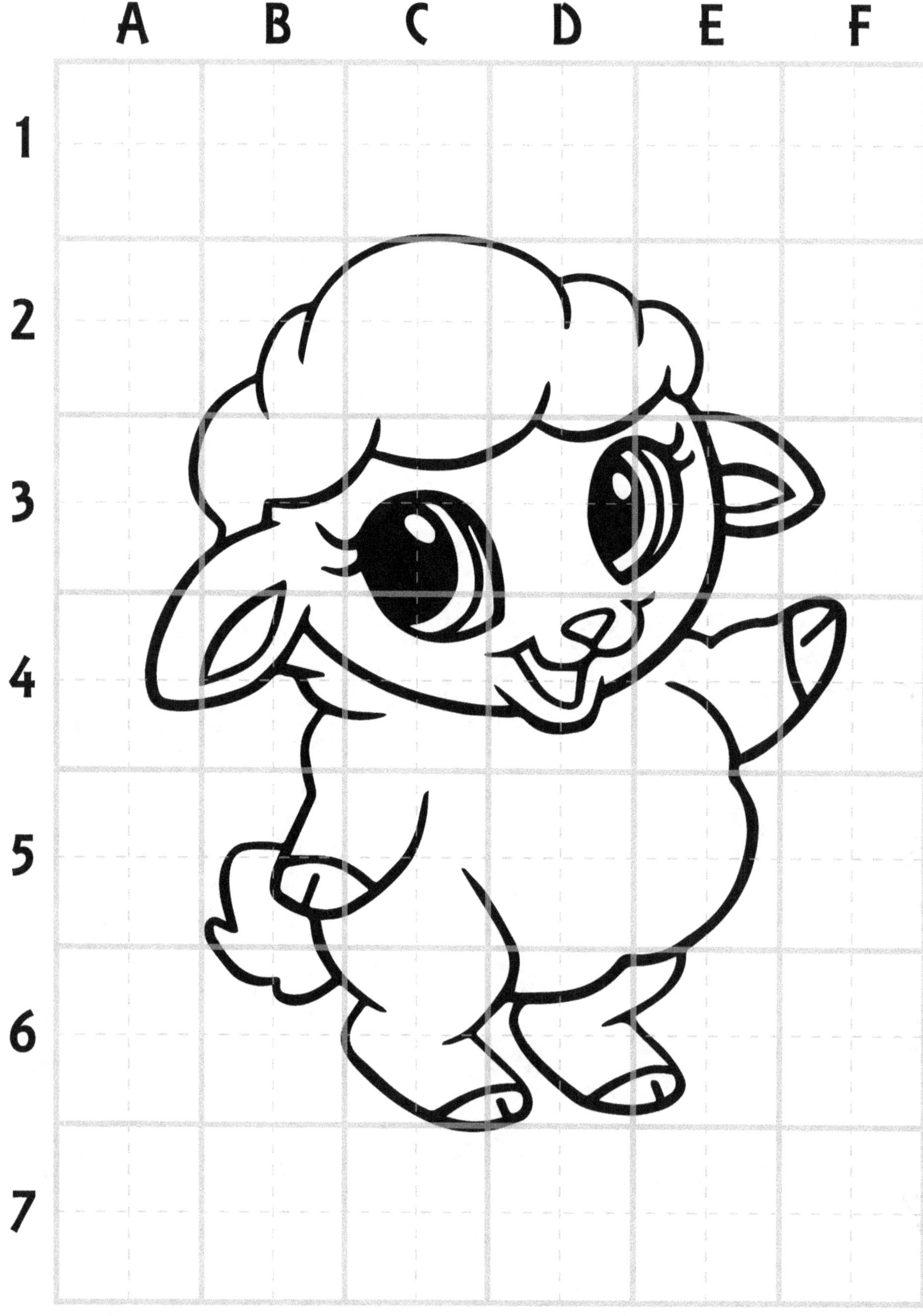

YOUR TURN!

<table>
<tr><td></td><td>A</td><td>B</td><td>C</td><td>D</td><td>E</td><td>F</td></tr>
<tr><td>1</td><td></td><td></td><td></td><td></td><td></td><td></td></tr>
<tr><td>2</td><td></td><td></td><td></td><td></td><td></td><td></td></tr>
<tr><td>3</td><td></td><td></td><td></td><td></td><td></td><td></td></tr>
<tr><td>4</td><td></td><td></td><td></td><td></td><td></td><td></td></tr>
<tr><td>5</td><td></td><td></td><td></td><td></td><td></td><td></td></tr>
<tr><td>6</td><td></td><td></td><td></td><td></td><td></td><td></td></tr>
<tr><td>7</td><td></td><td></td><td></td><td></td><td></td><td></td></tr>
</table>

HORSE

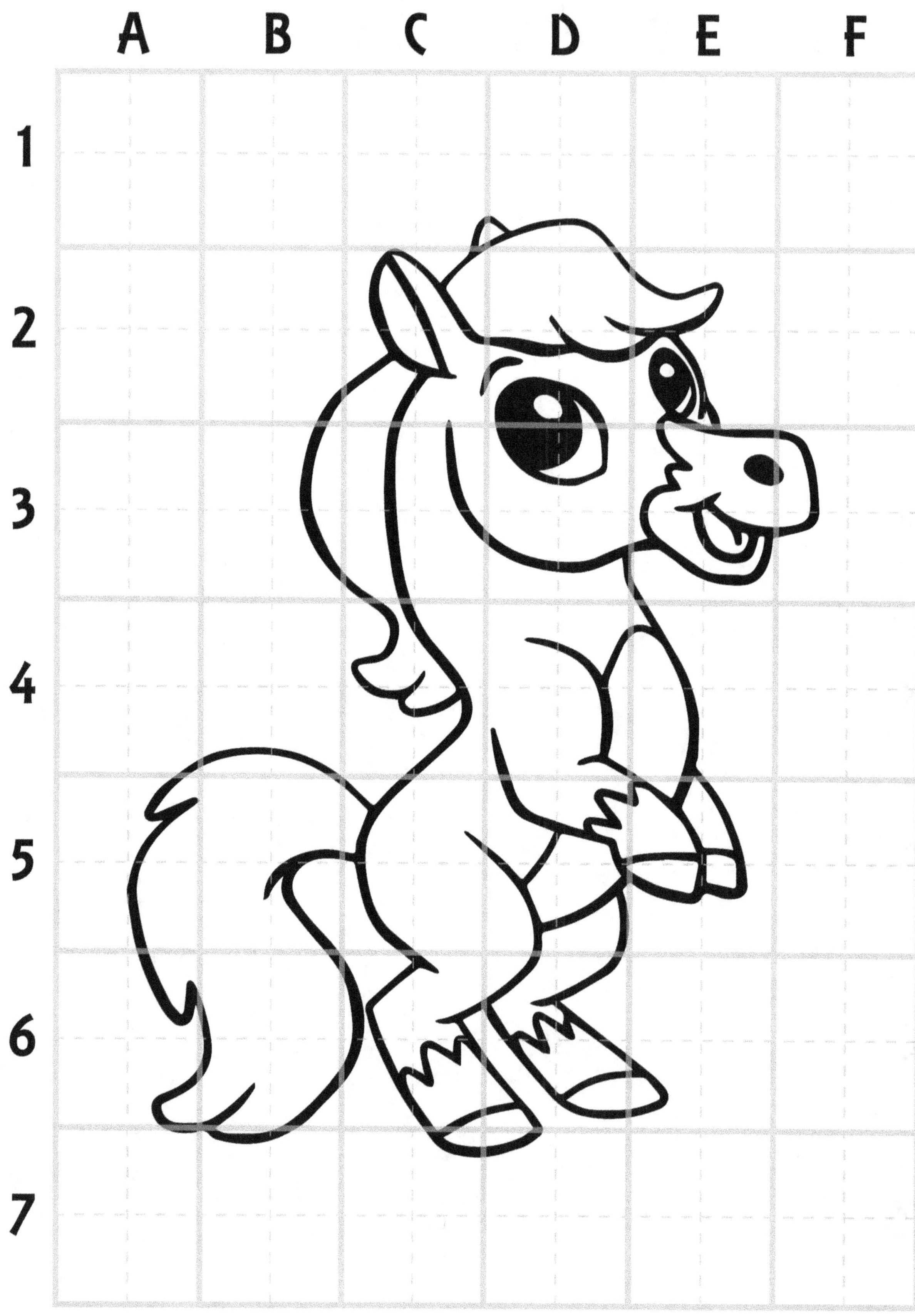

YOUR TURN!

	A	B	C	D	E	F
1						
2						
3						
4						
5						
6						
7						

PIG

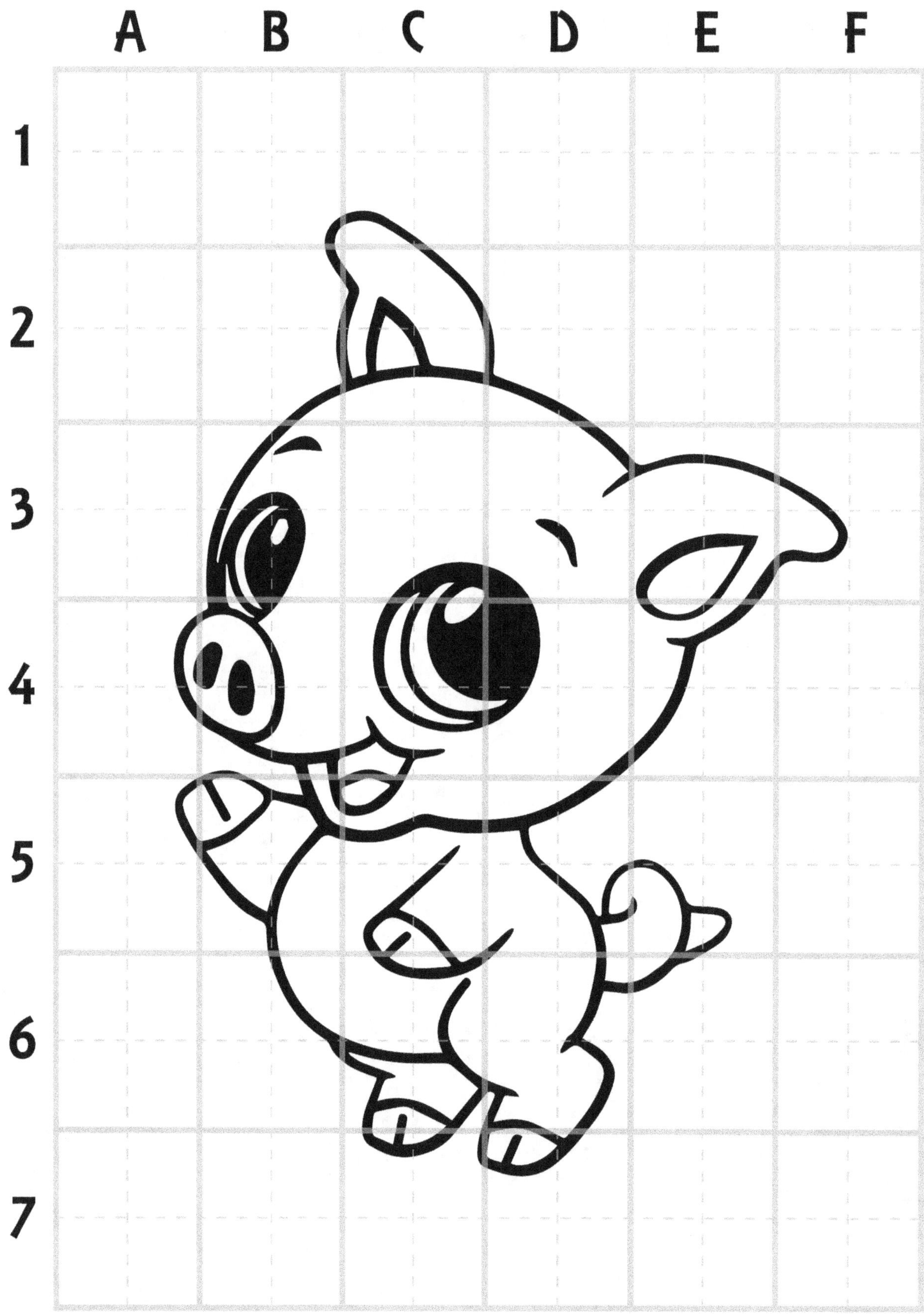

YOUR TURN!

	A	B	C	D	E	F
1						
2						
3						
4						
5						
6						
7						

BIGHORN SHEEP

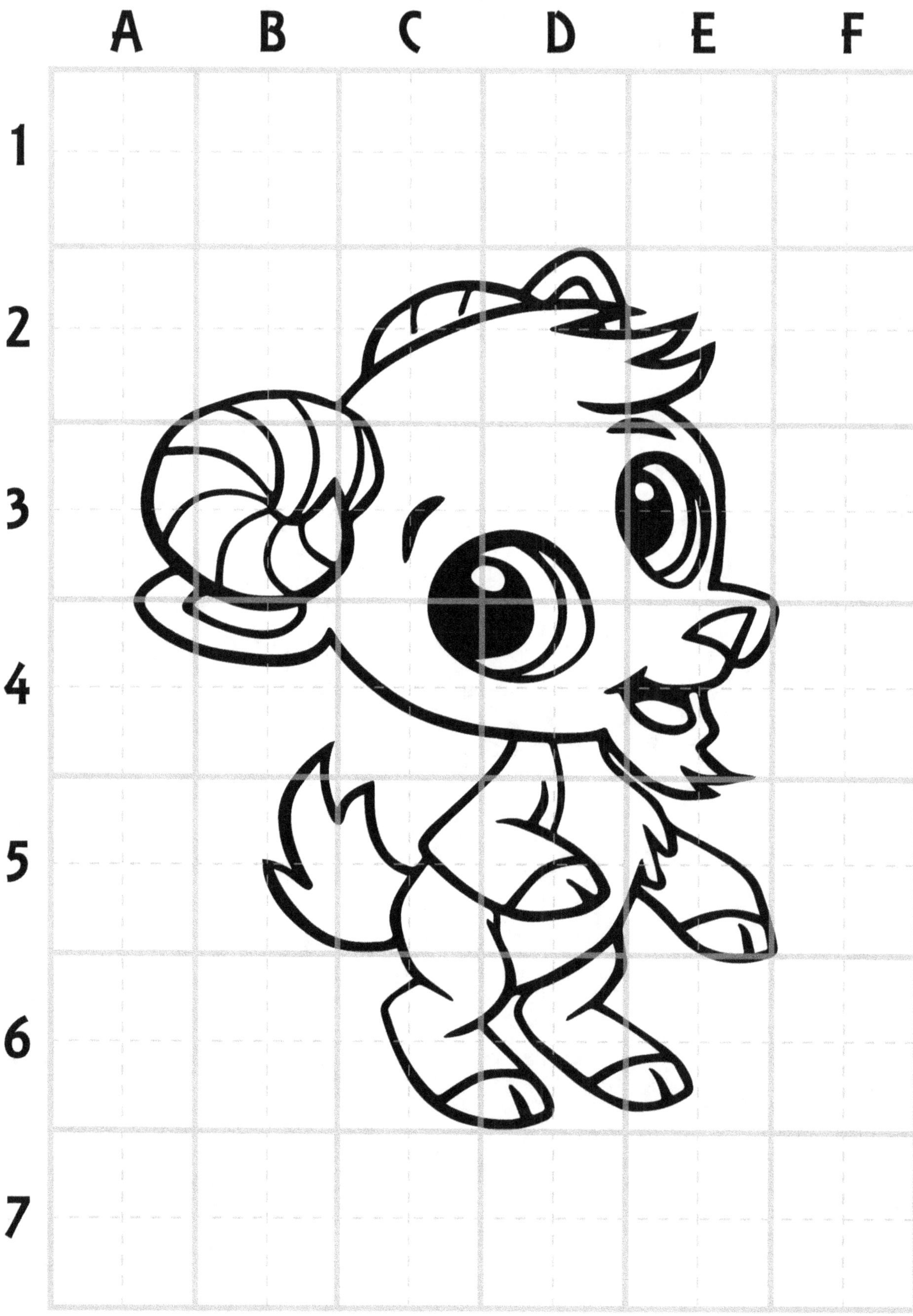

YOUR TURN!

	A	B	C	D	E	F
1						
2						
3						
4						
5						
6						
7						

BIRD

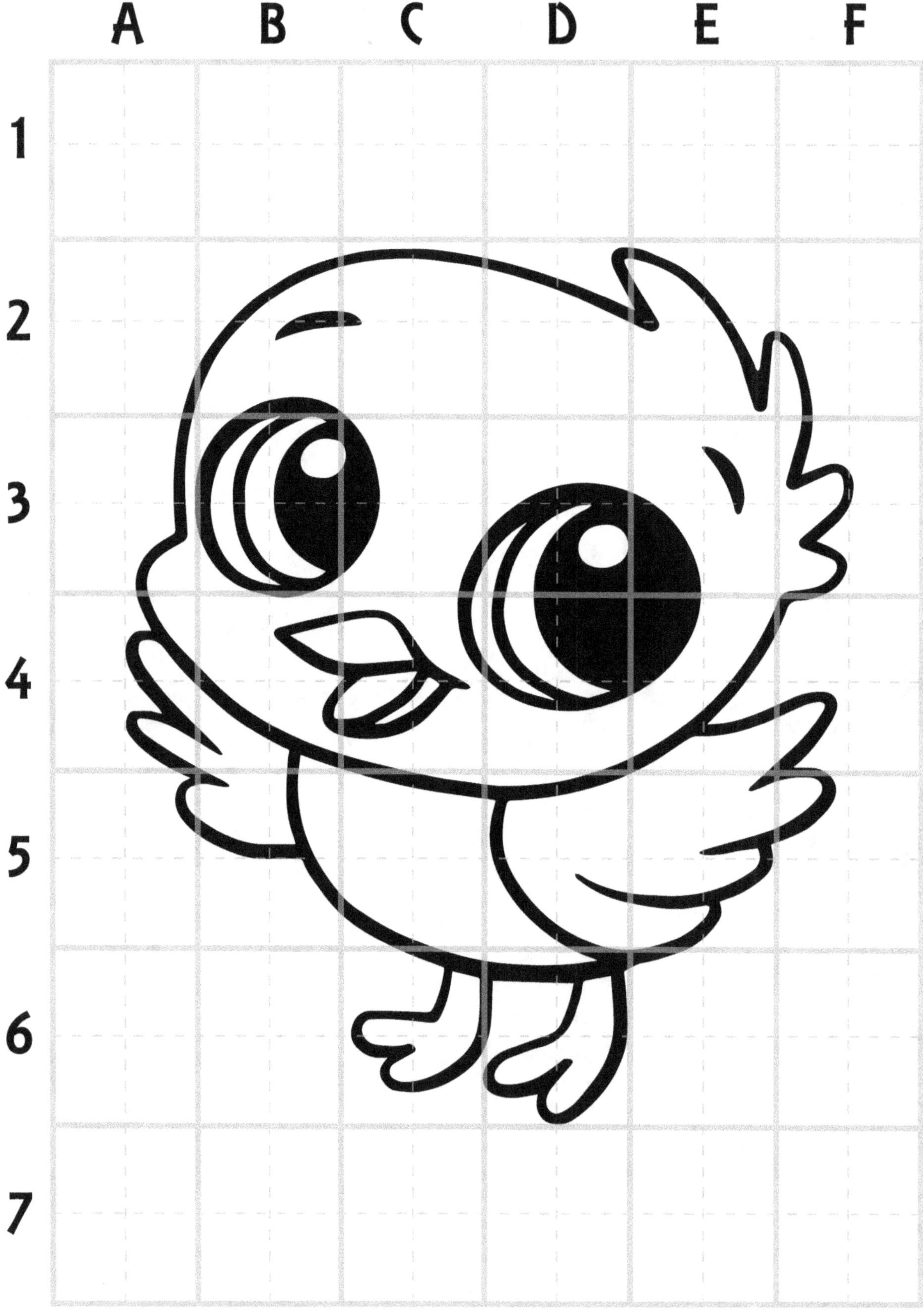

YOUR TURN!

	A	B	C	D	E	F
1						
2						
3						
4						
5						
6						
7						

TURTLE

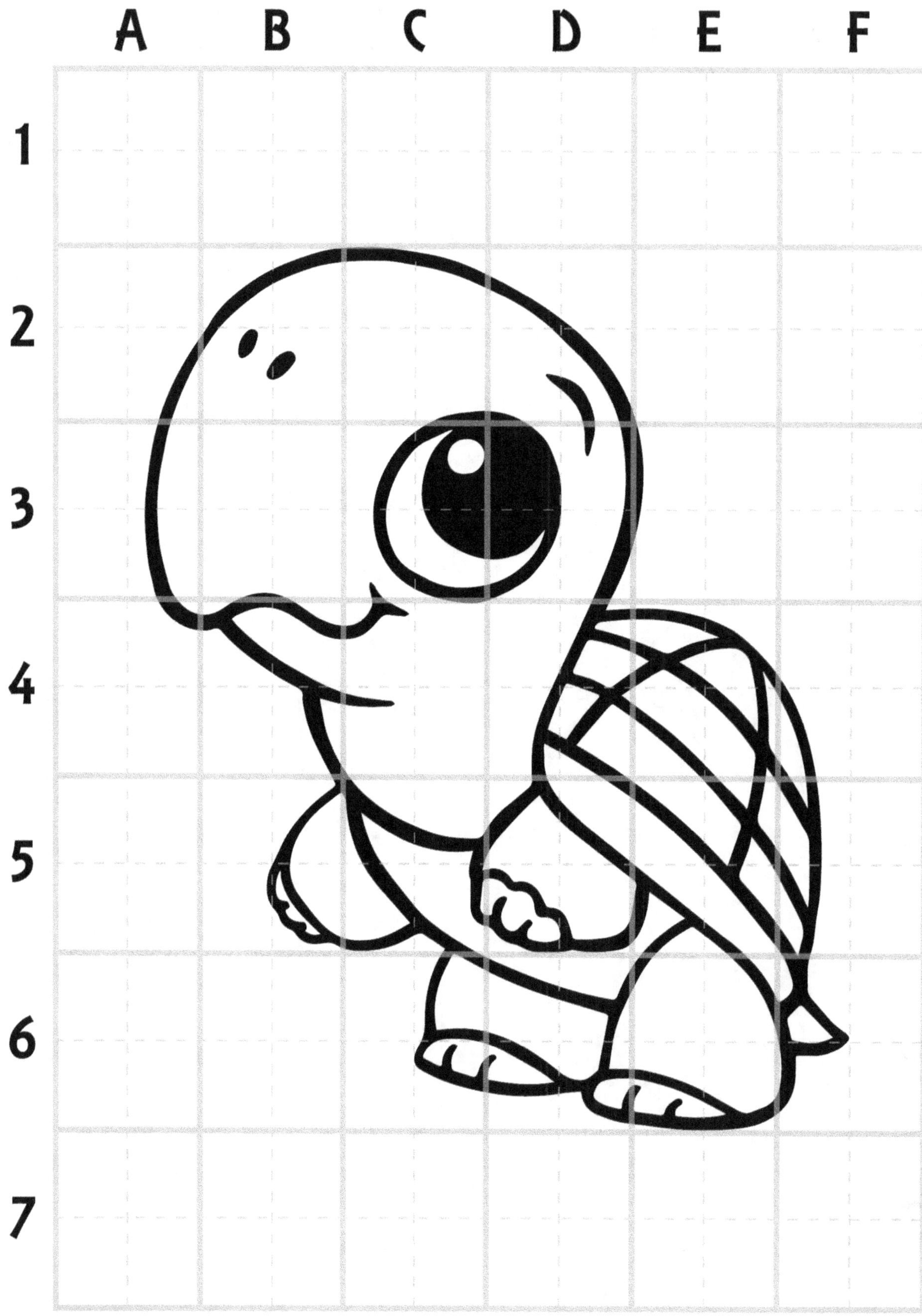

YOUR TURN!

	A	B	C	D	E	F
1						
2						
3						
4						
5						
6						
7						

TIGER

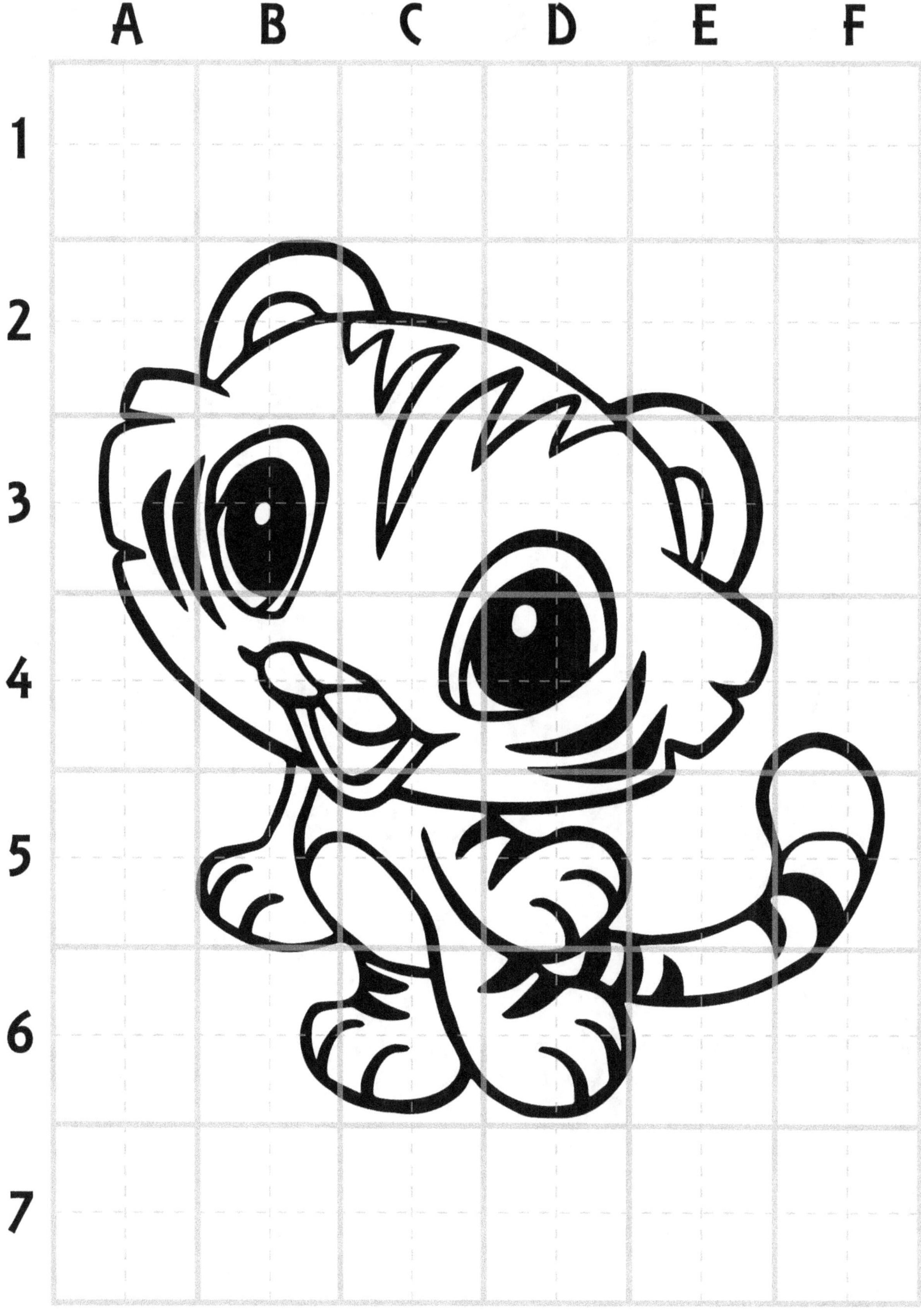

YOUR TURN!

	A	B	C	D	E	F
1						
2						
3						
4						
5						
6						
7						

HIPPO

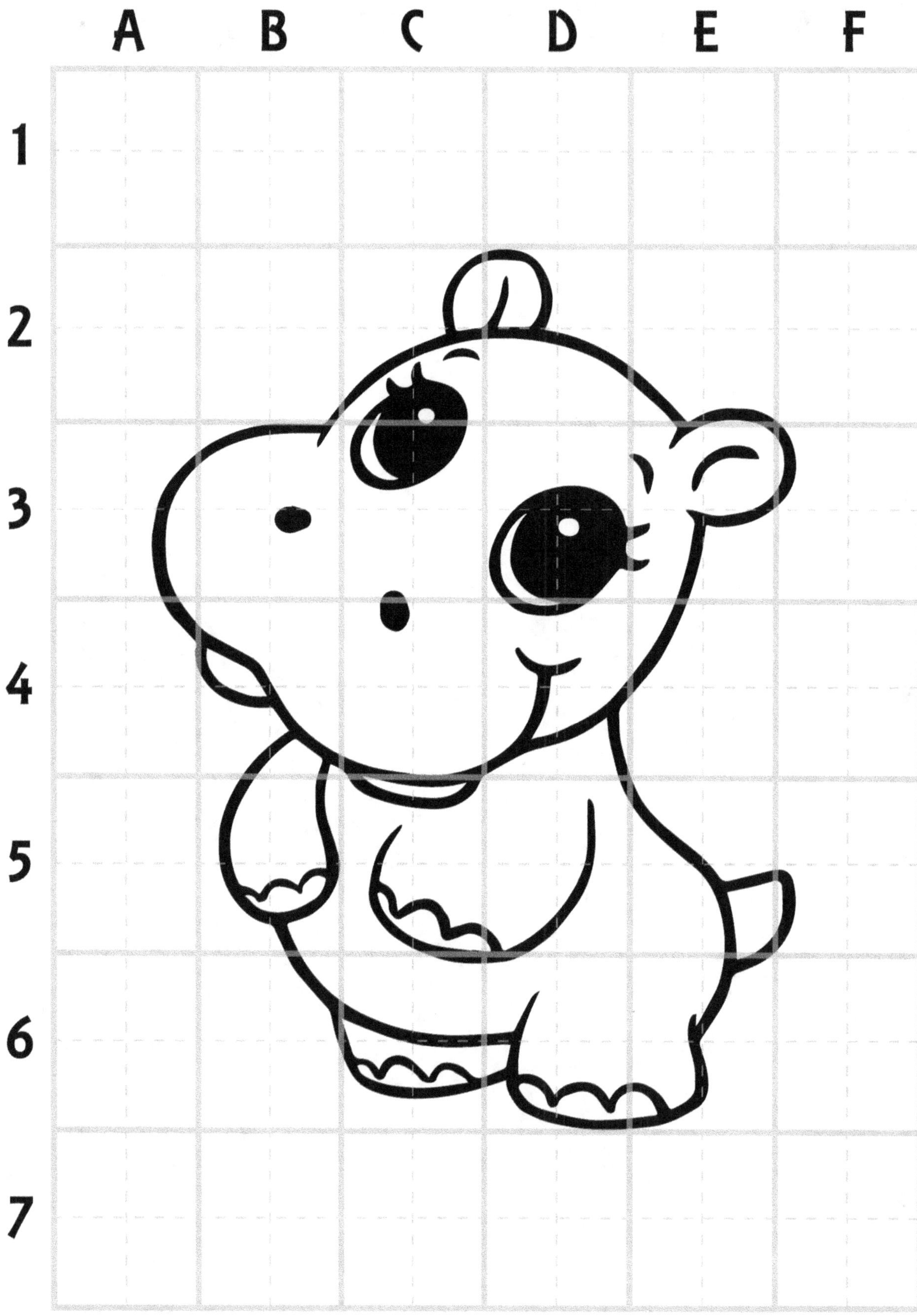

YOUR TURN!

	A	B	C	D	E	F
1						
2						
3						
4						
5						
6						
7						

COW

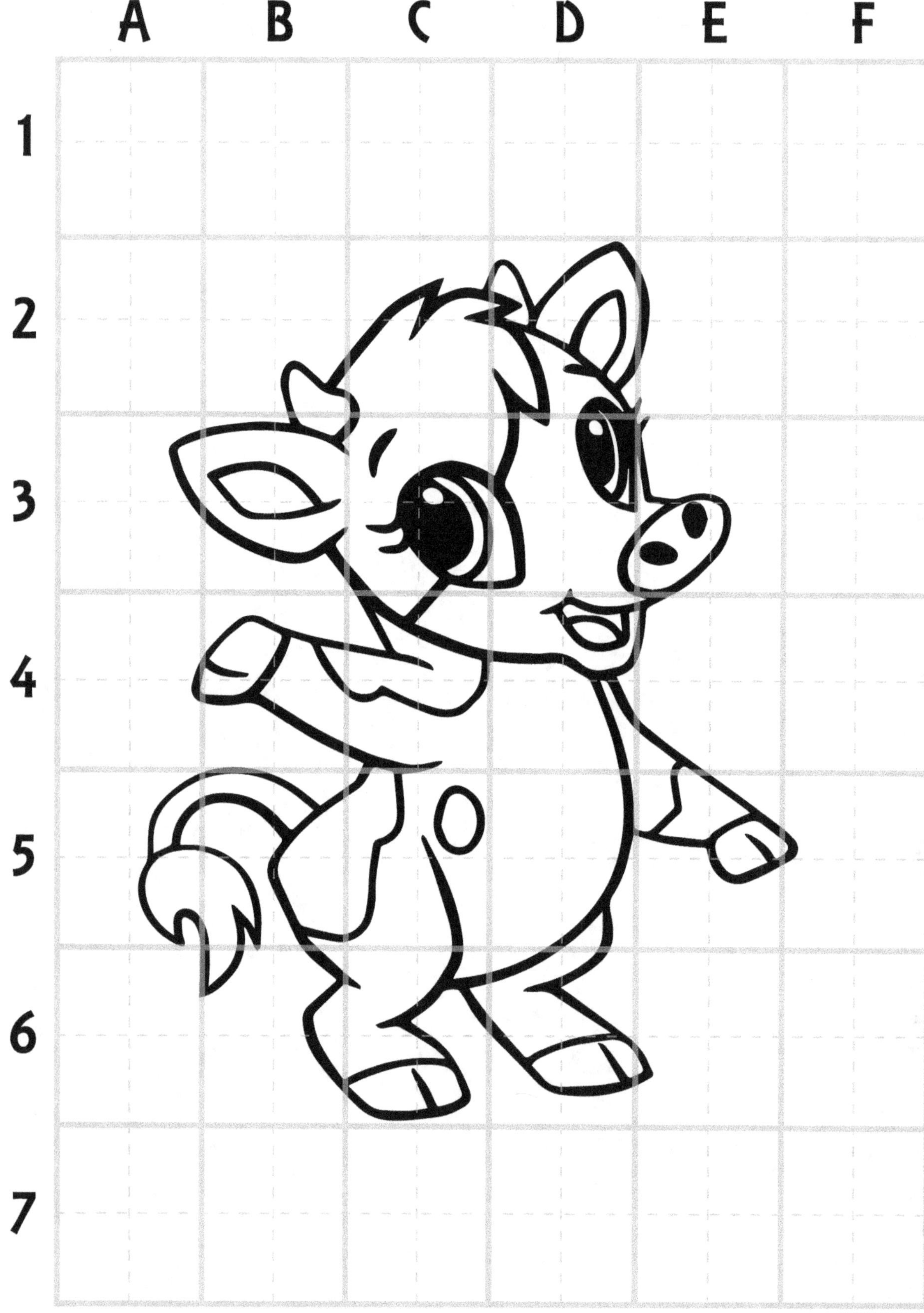

YOUR TURN!

	A	B	C	D	E	F
1						
2						
3						
4						
5						
6						
7						

TEDDY BEAR

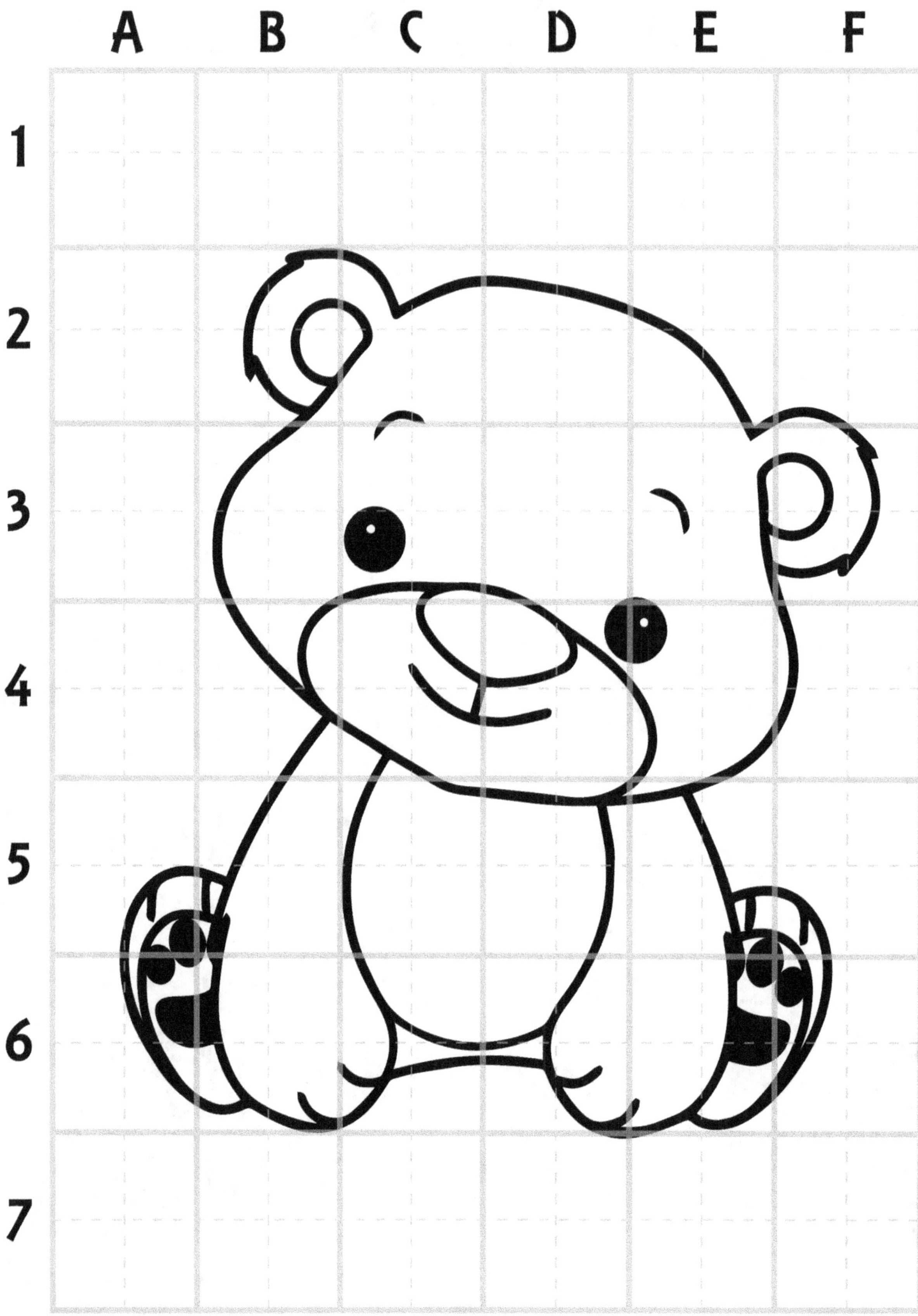

YOUR TURN!

	A	B	C	D	E	F
1						
2						
3						
4						
5						
6						
7						

DESSIN SINGE

A   B   C   D   E   F

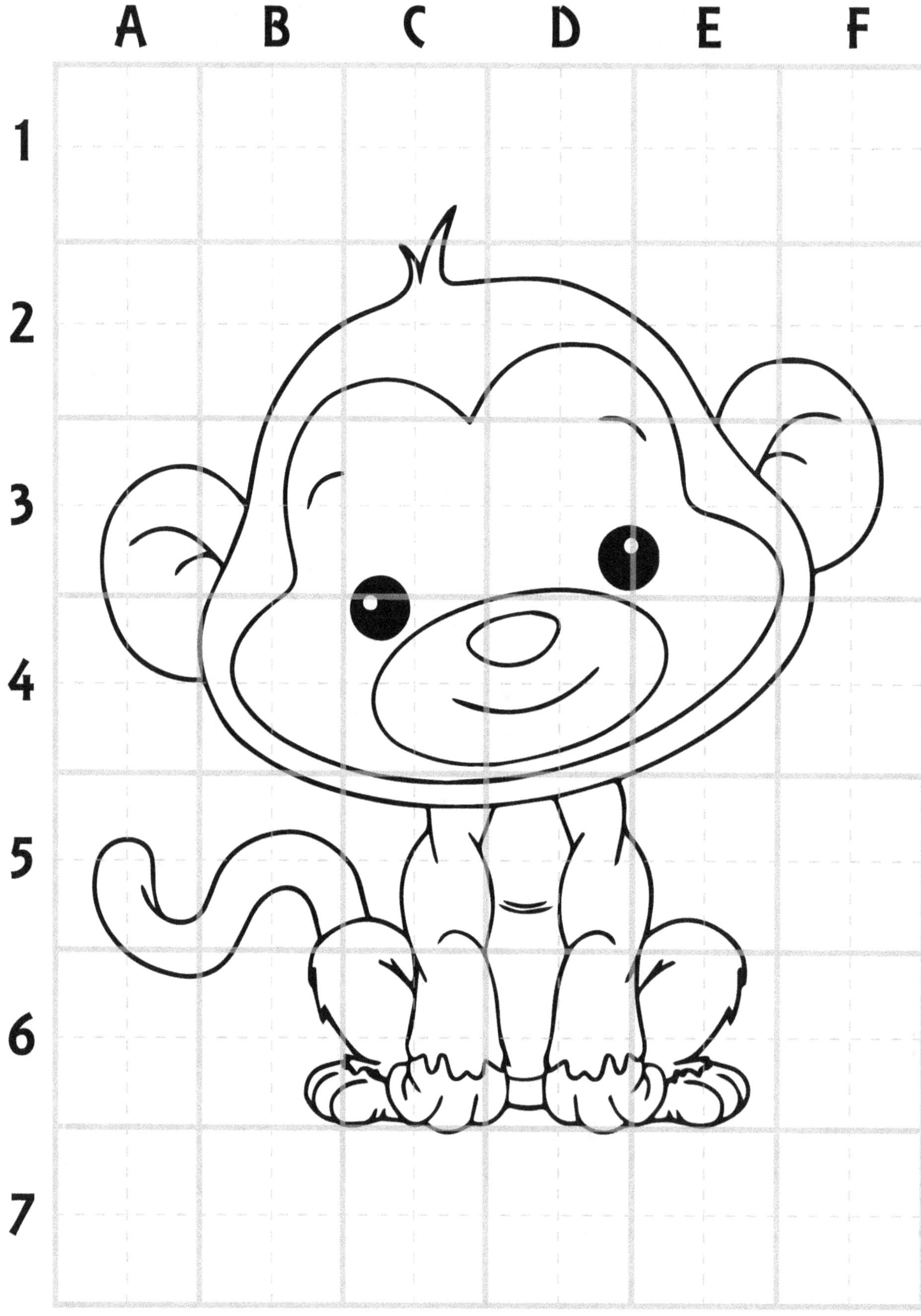

YOUR TURN!

	A	B	C	D	E	F
1						
2						
3						
4						
5						
6						
7						

ELEPHANT

A B C D E F

1

2

3

4

5

6

7

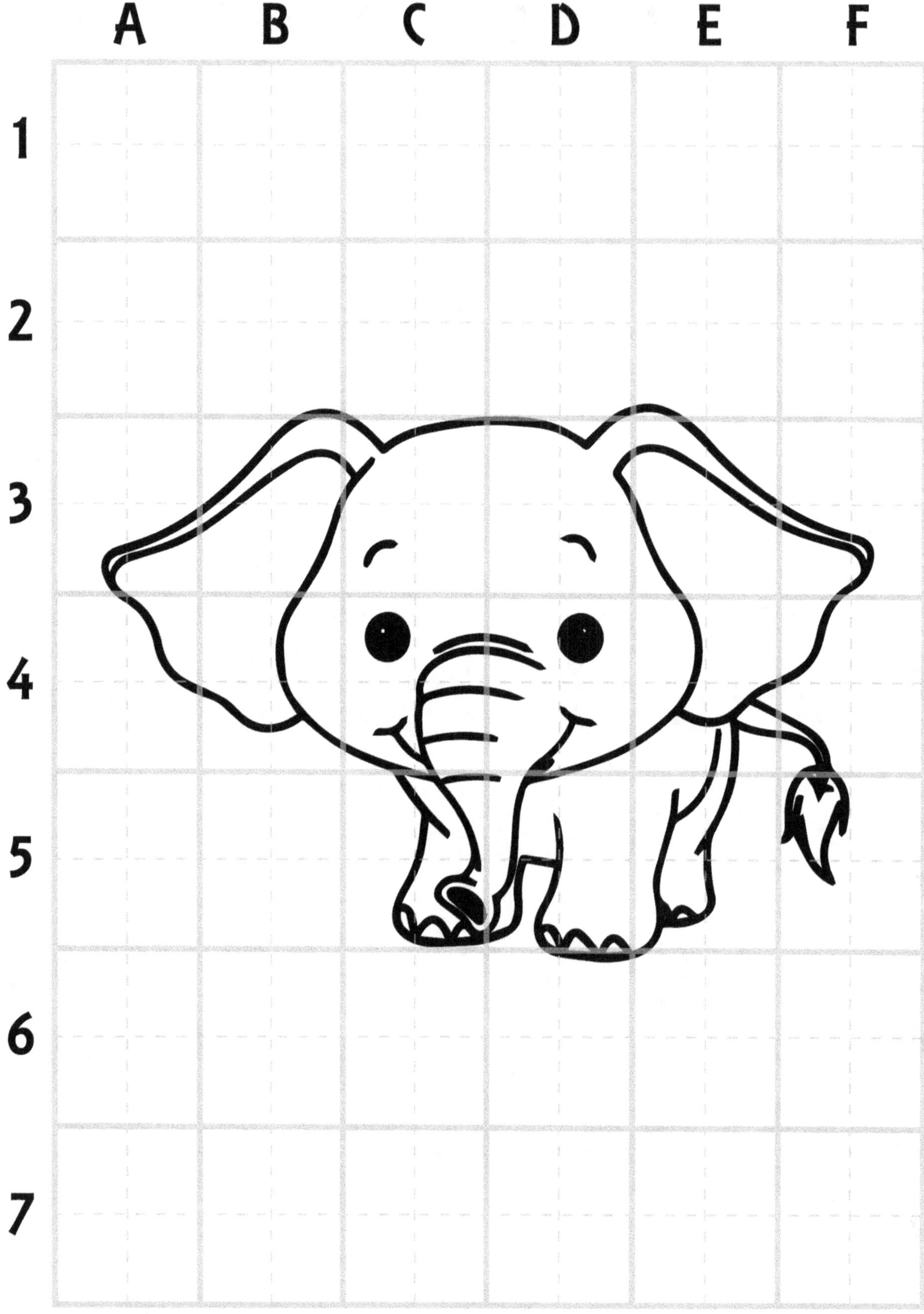

YOUR TURN!

	A	B	C	D	E	F
1						
2						
3						
4						
5						
6						
7						

GIRAFFE

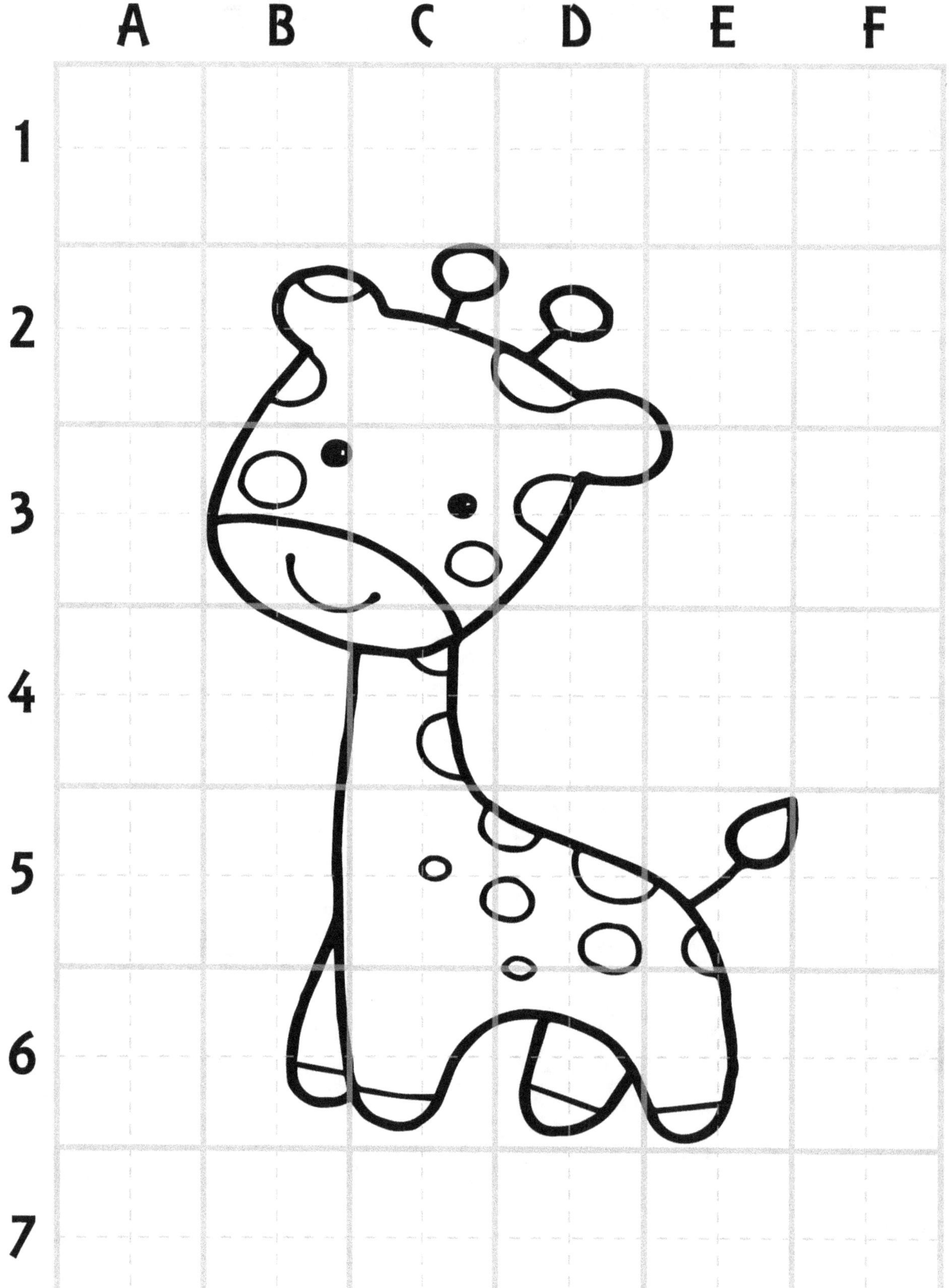

YOUR TURN!

	A	B	C	D	E	F
1						
2						
3						
4						
5						
6						
7						

BAT

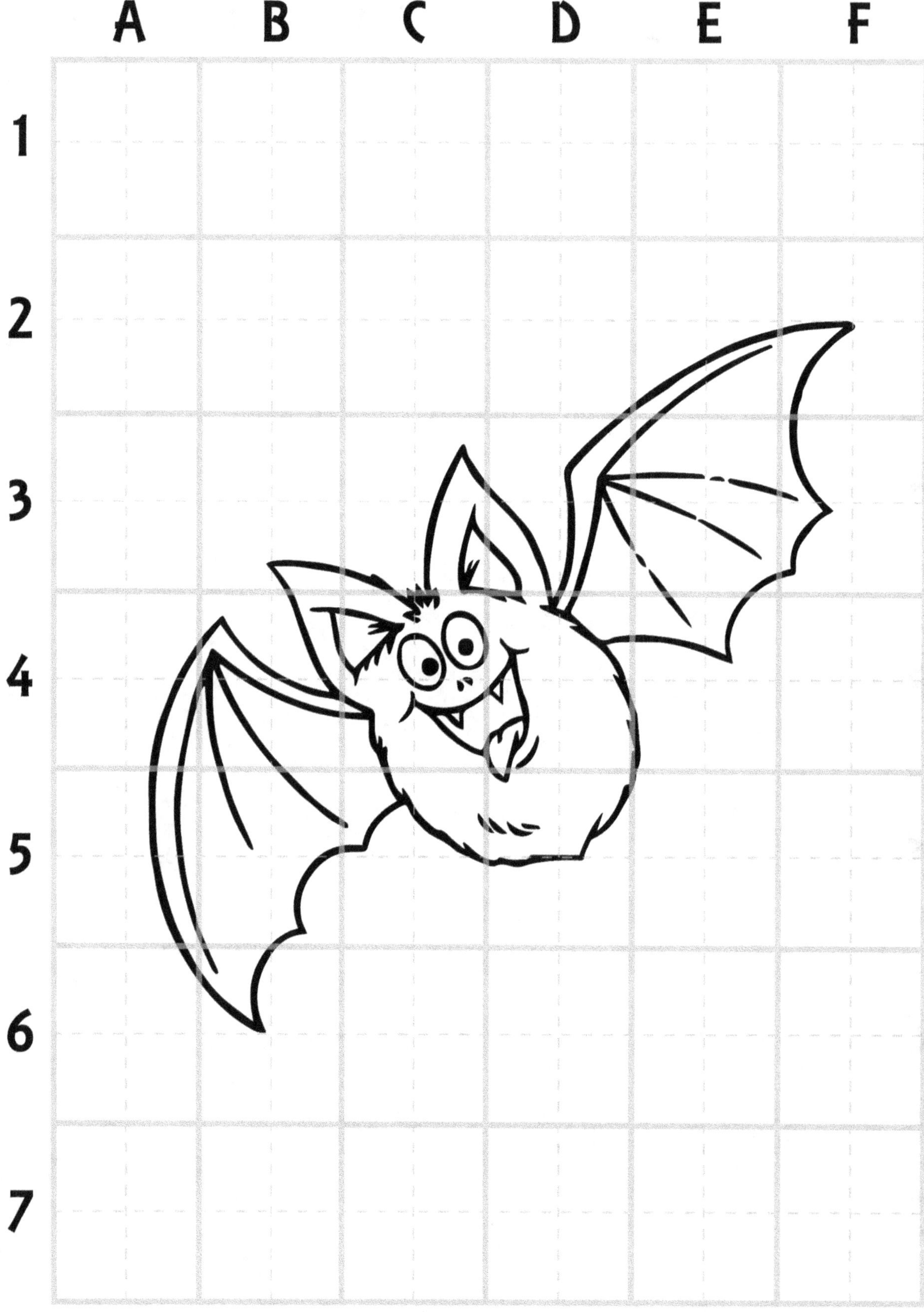

YOUR TURN!

	A	B	C	D	E	F
1						
2						
3						
4						
5						
6						
7						

DUCK

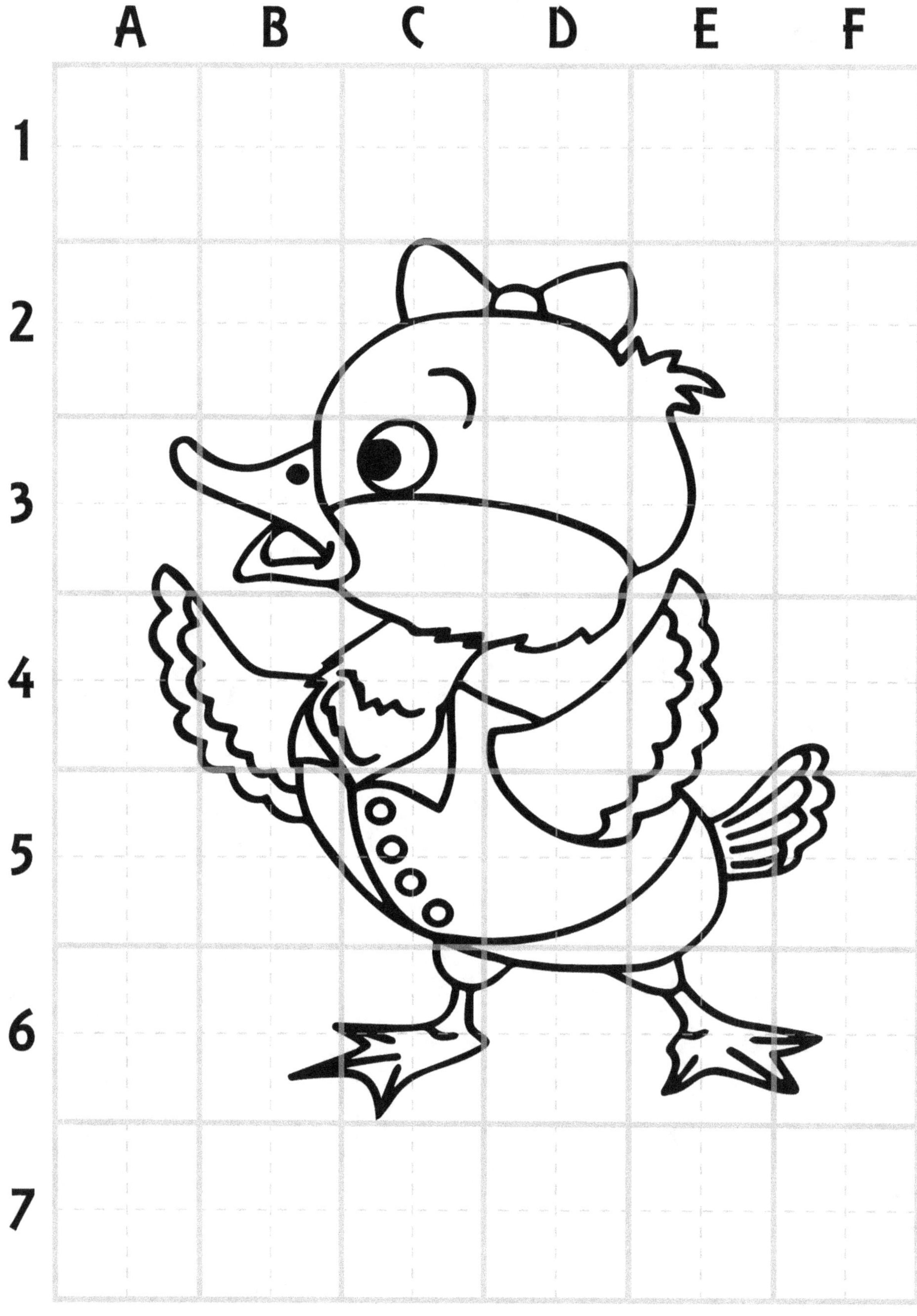

YOUR TURN!

	A	B	C	D	E	F
1						
2						
3						
4						
5						
6						
7						

FROG

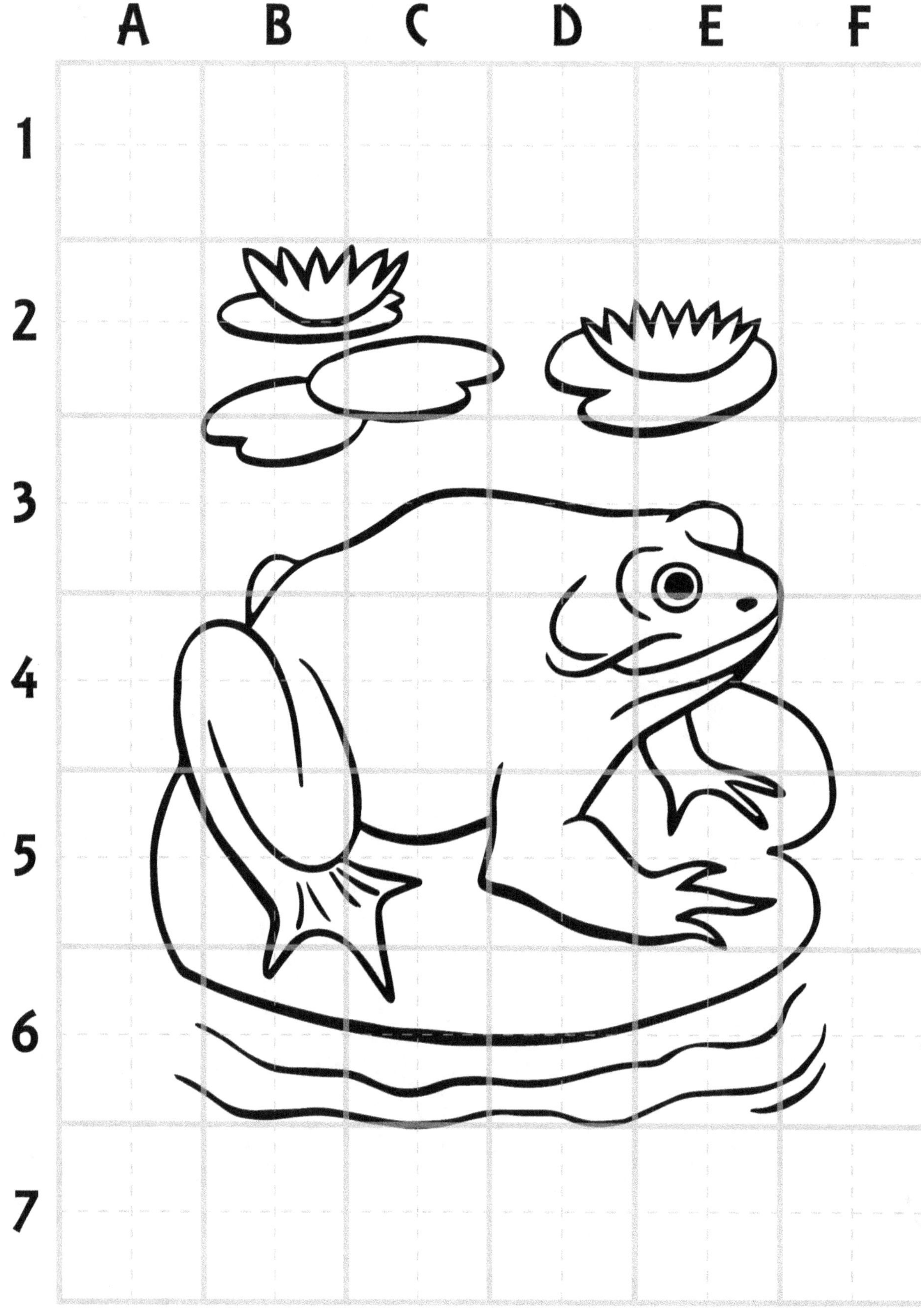

YOUR TURN!

	A	B	C	D	E	F
1						
2						
3						
4						
5						
6						
7						

CAT

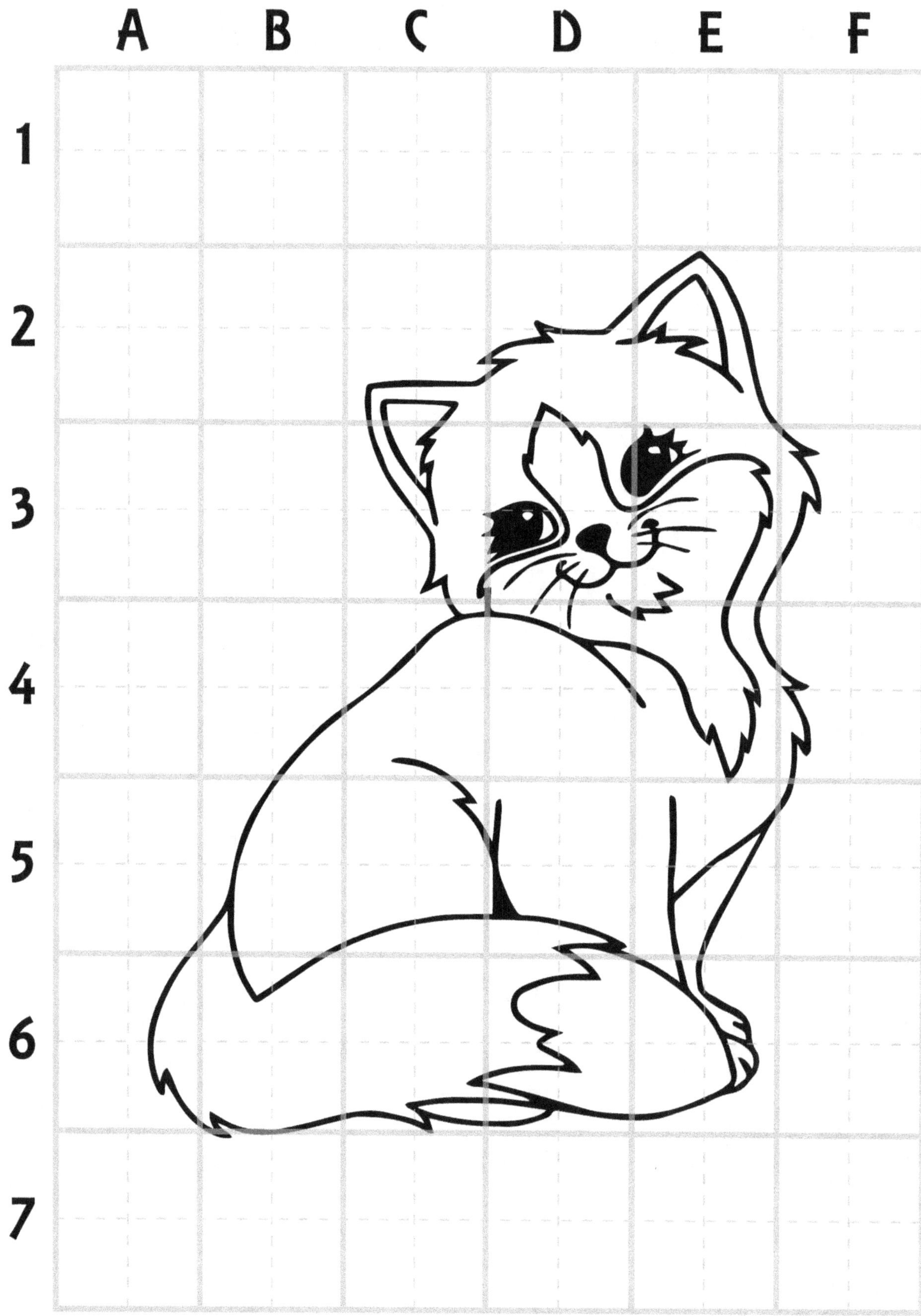

YOUR TURN!

	A	B	C	D	E	F
1						
2						
3						
4						
5						
6						
7						

HIPPO

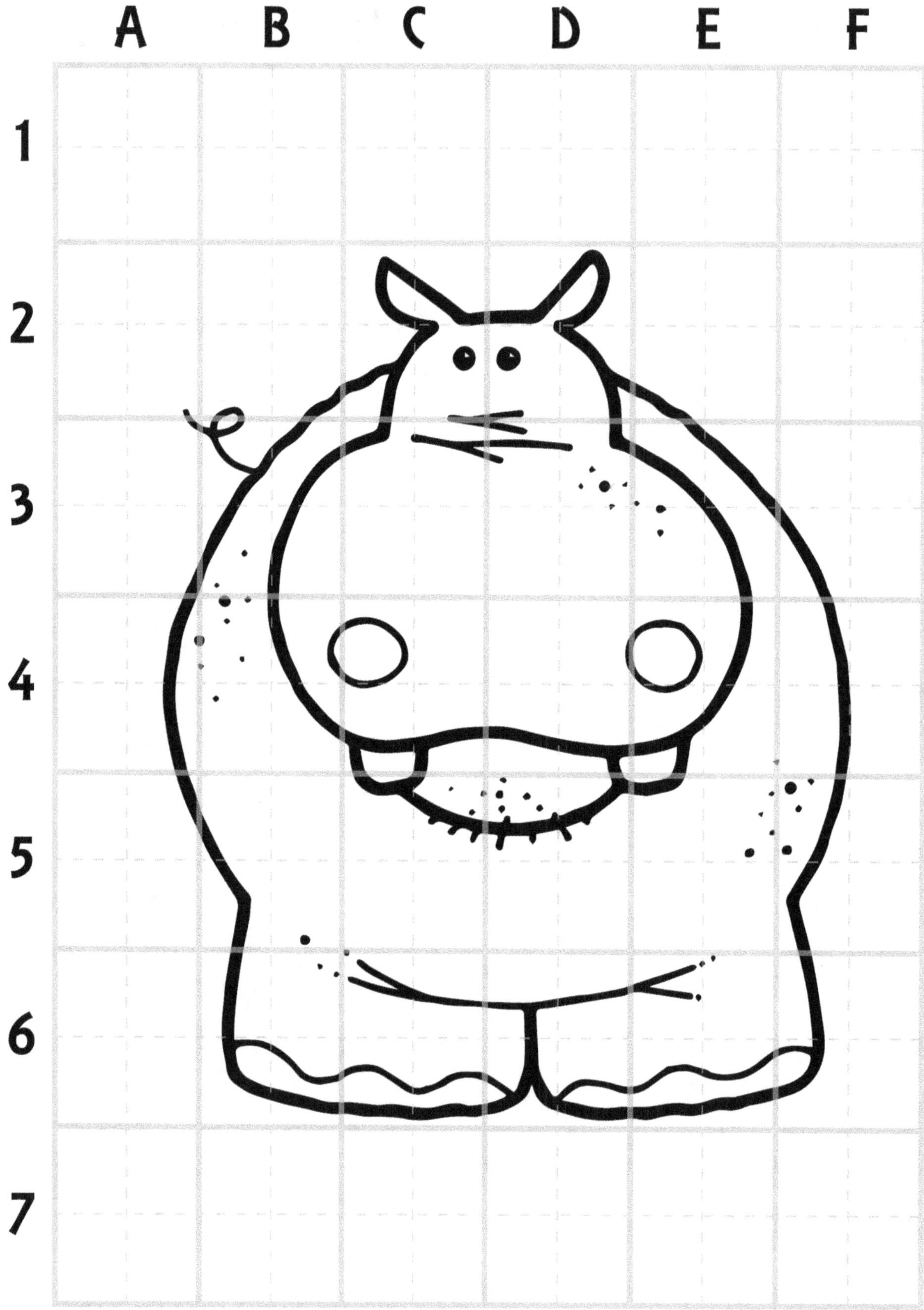

YOUR TURN!

	A	B	C	D	E	F
1						
2						
3						
4						
5						
6						
7						

BUTTERFLY

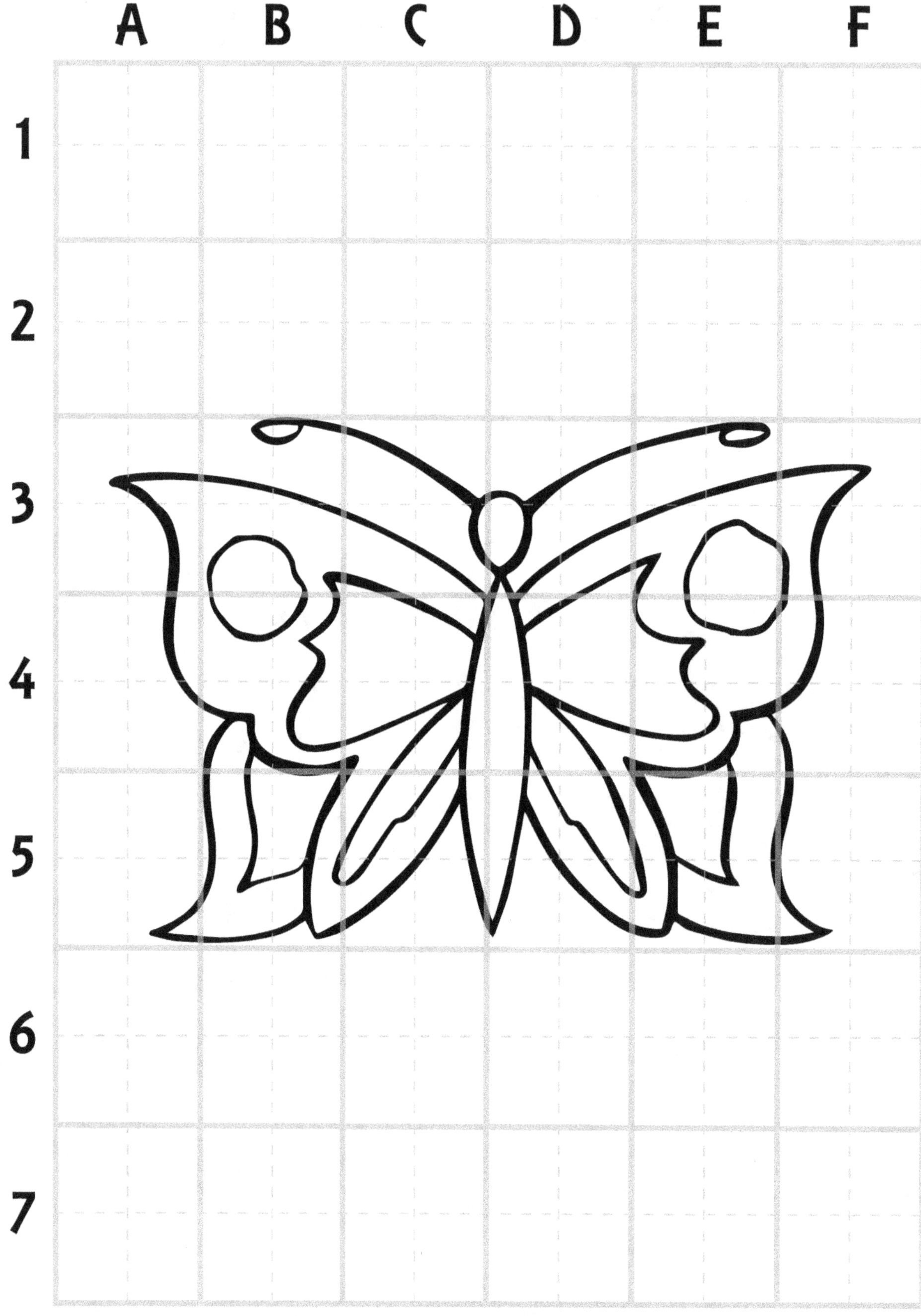

YOUR TURN!

	A	B	C	D	E	F
1						
2						
3						
4						
5						
6						
7						

MONKEY

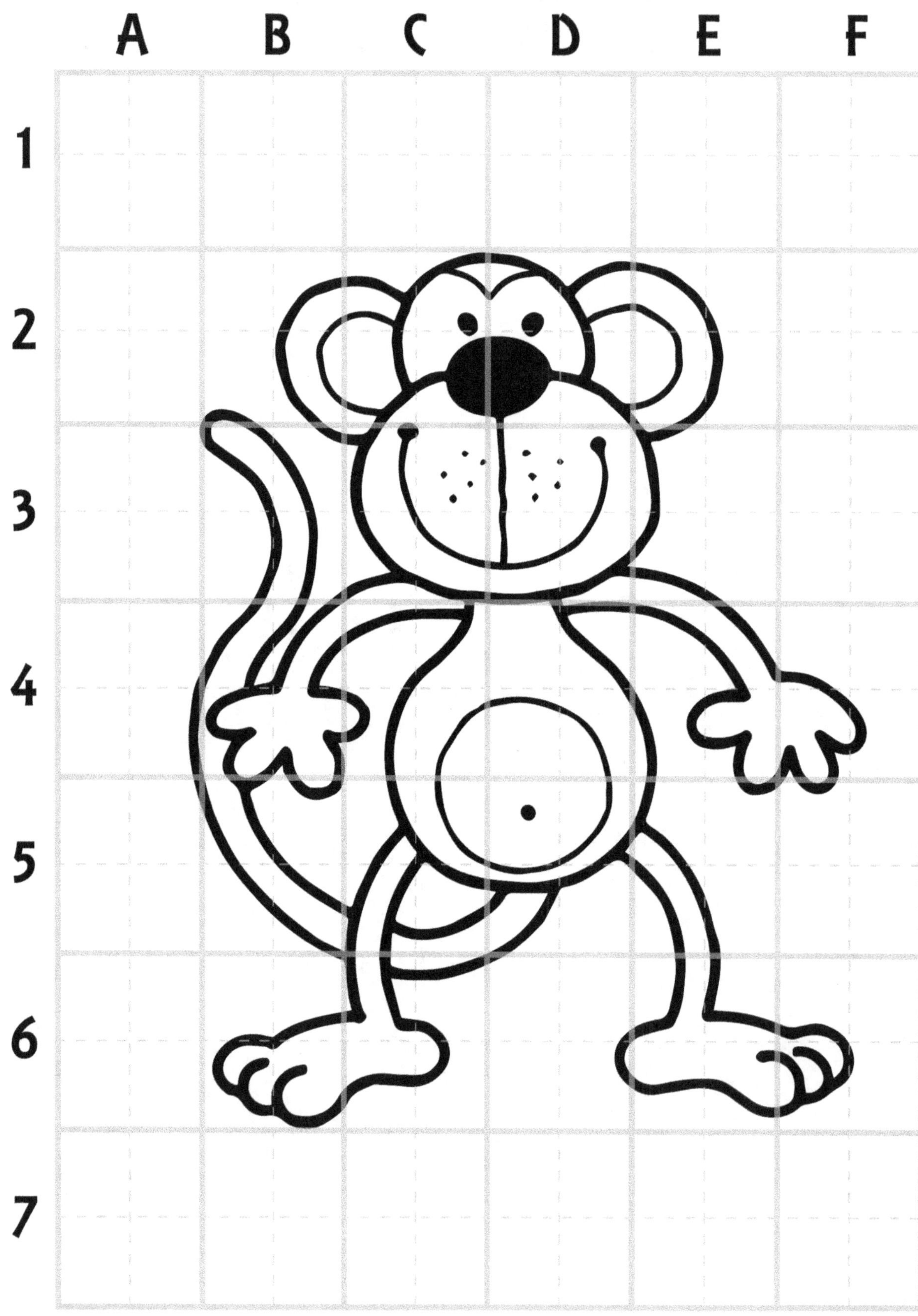

YOUR TURN!

	A	B	C	D	E	F
1						
2						
3						
4						
5						
6						
7						

MACAW

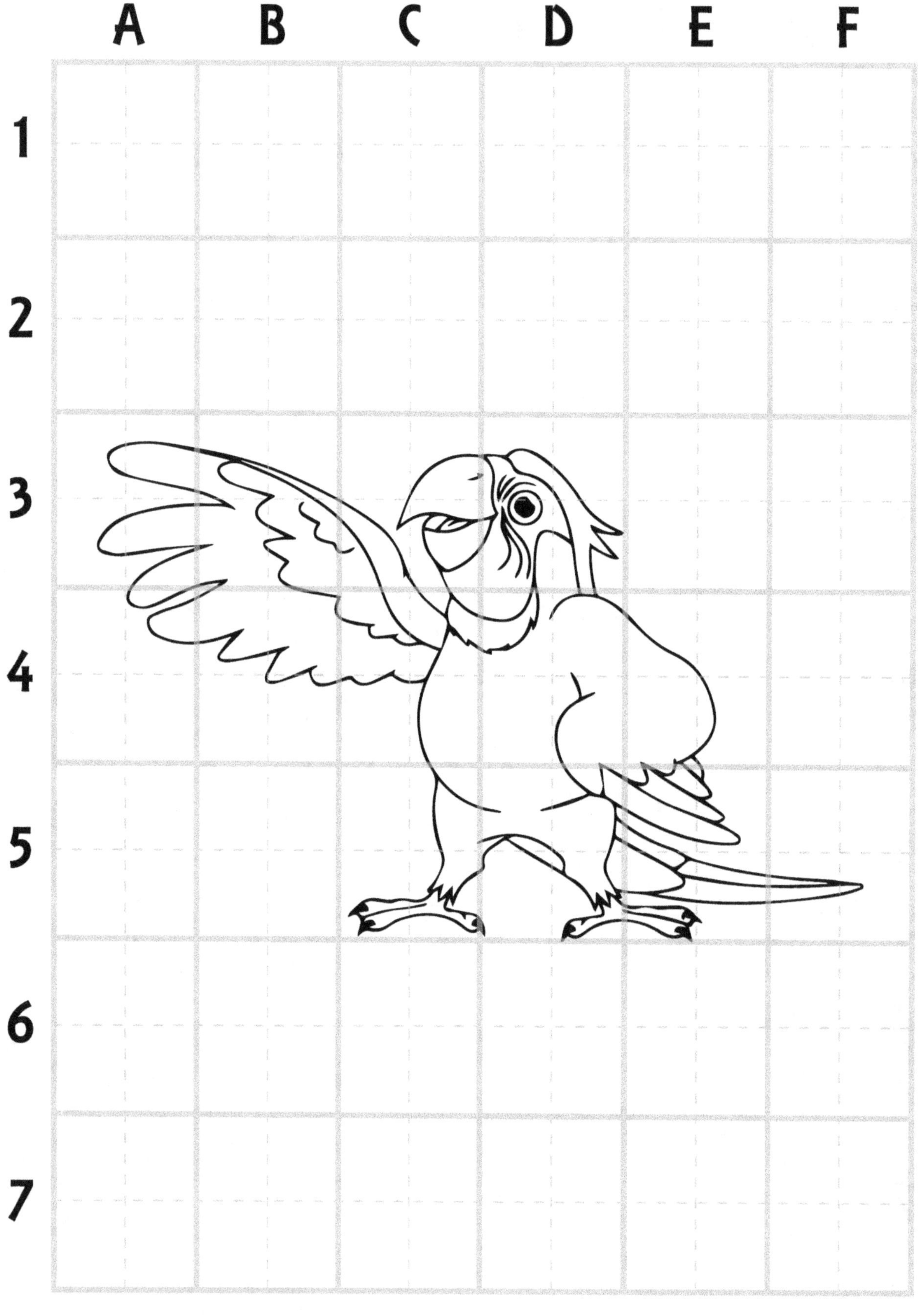

YOUR TURN!

	A	B	C	D	E	F
1						
2						
3						
4						
5						
6						
7						

BEAR

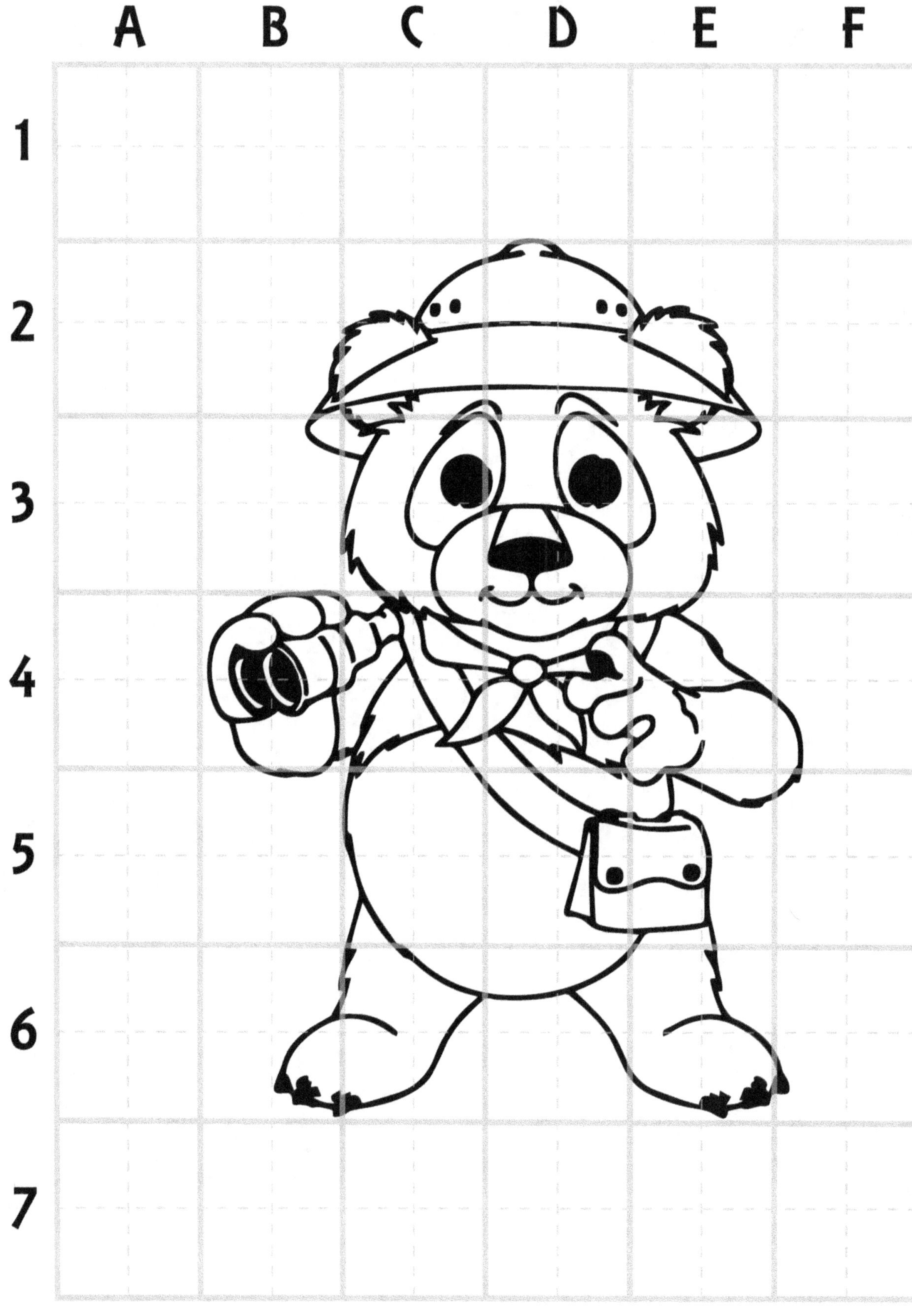

YOUR TURN!

	A	B	C	D	E	F
1						
2						
3						
4						
5						
6						
7						

DOLPHIN

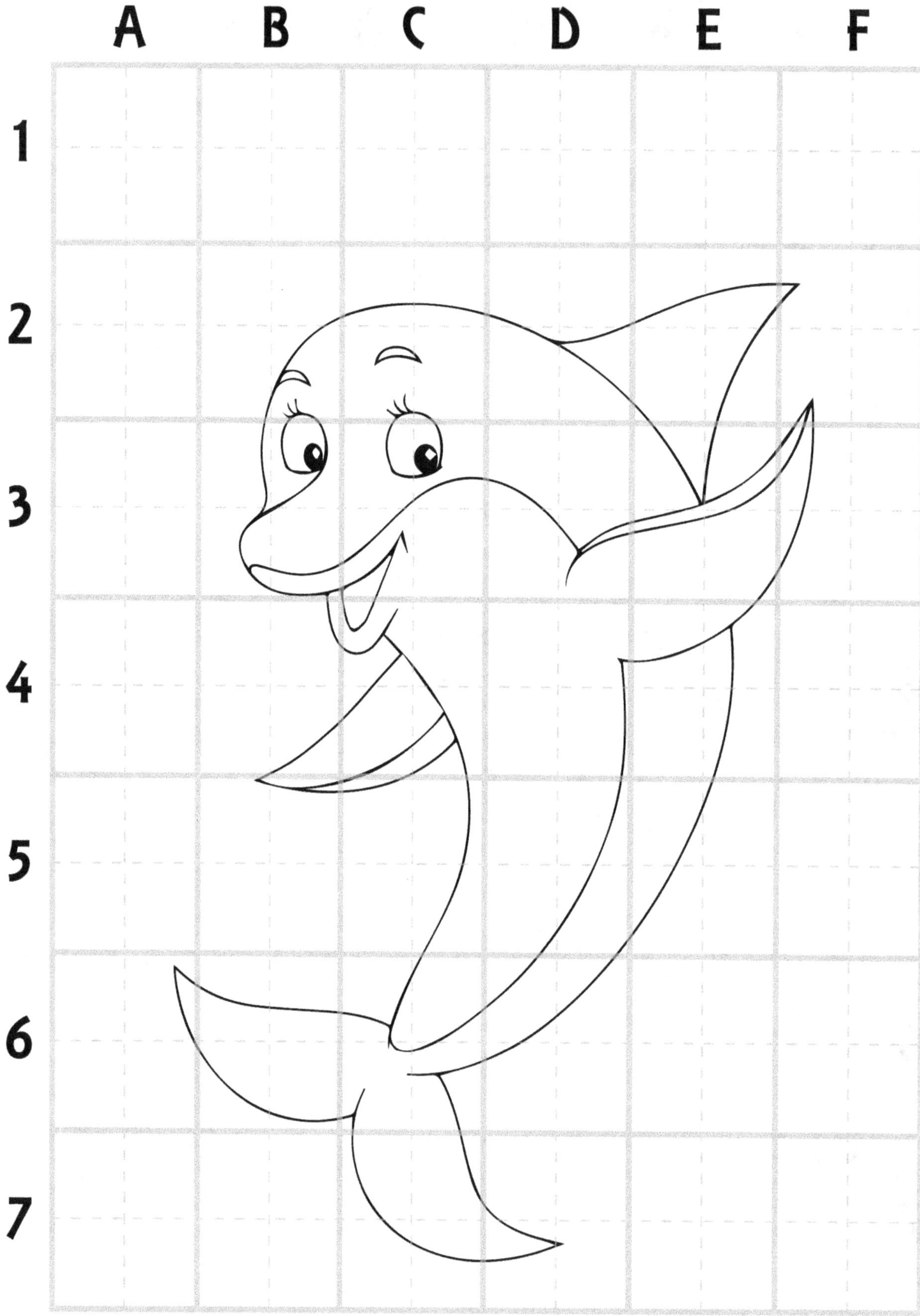

YOUR TURN!

	A	B	C	D	E	F
1						
2						
3						
4						
5						
6						
7						

FROG

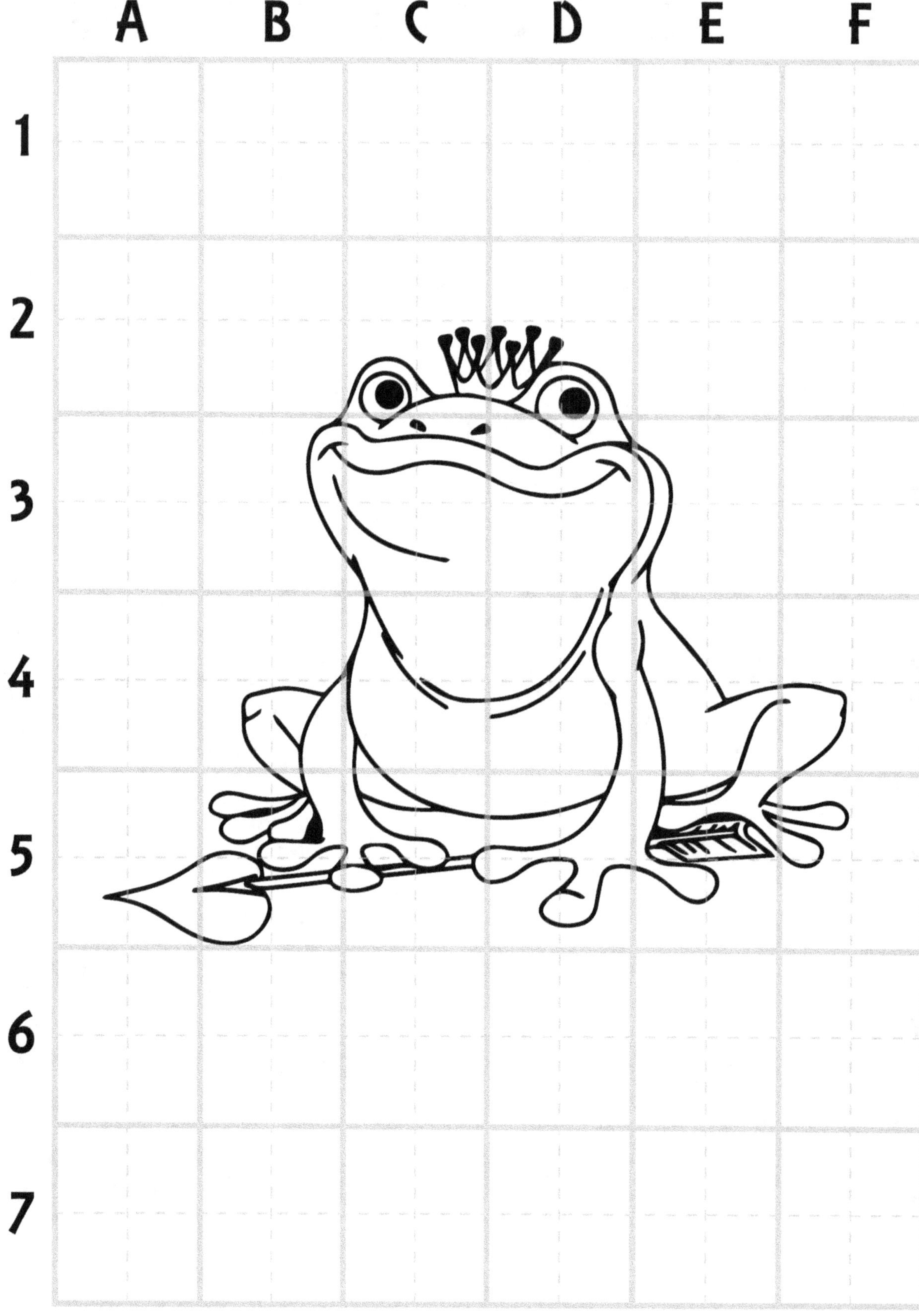

YOUR TURN!

	A	B	C	D	E	F
1						
2						
3						
4						
5						
6						
7						

GOAT

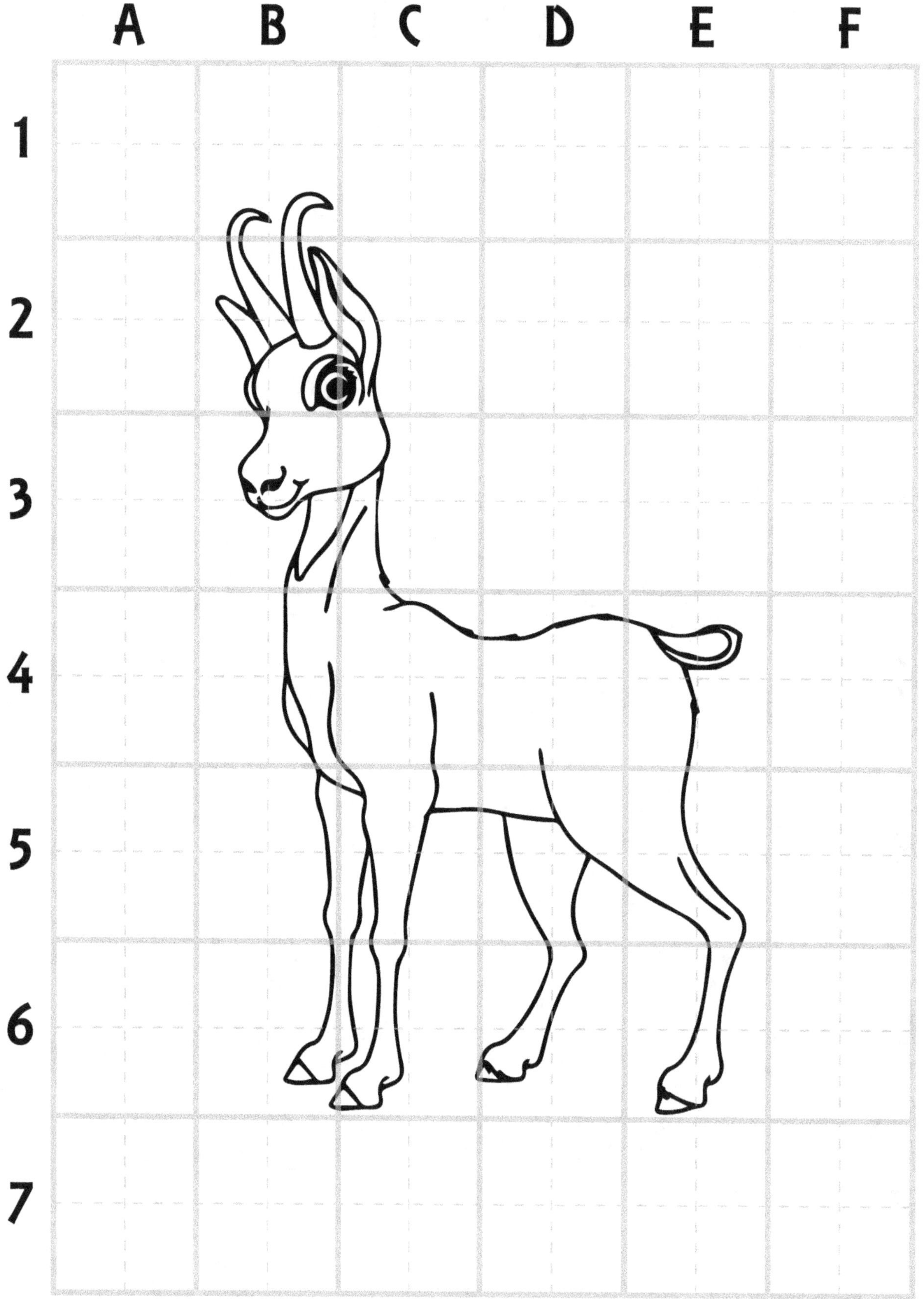

A B C D E F

1
2
3
4
5
6
7

YOUR TURN!

	A	B	C	D	E	F
1						
2						
3						
4						
5						
6						
7						

PEACOCK

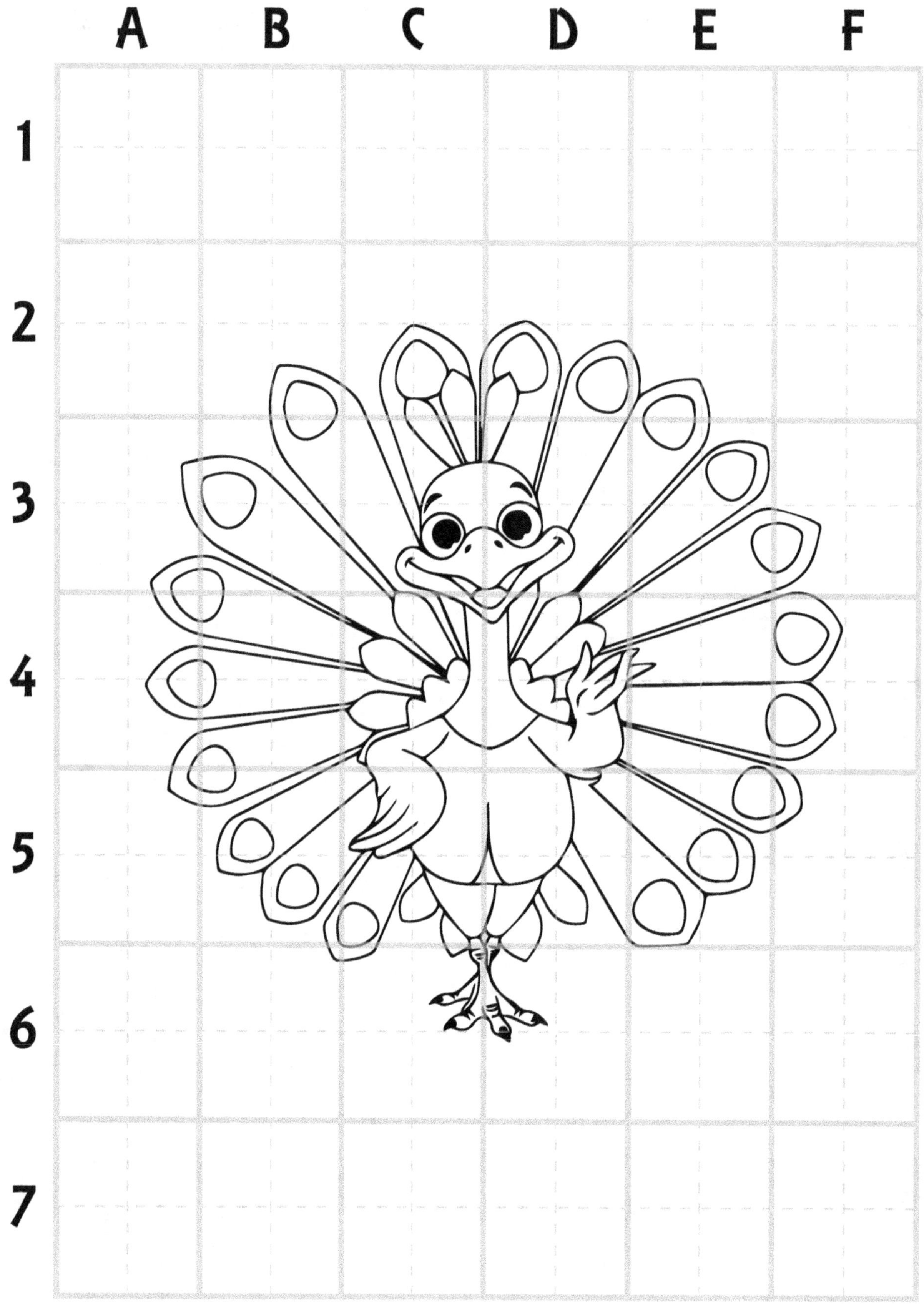

	A	B	C	D	E	F
1						
2						
3						
4						
5						
6						
7						

YOUR TURN!

	A	B	C	D	E	F
1						
2						
3						
4						
5						
6						
7						

TURTLE

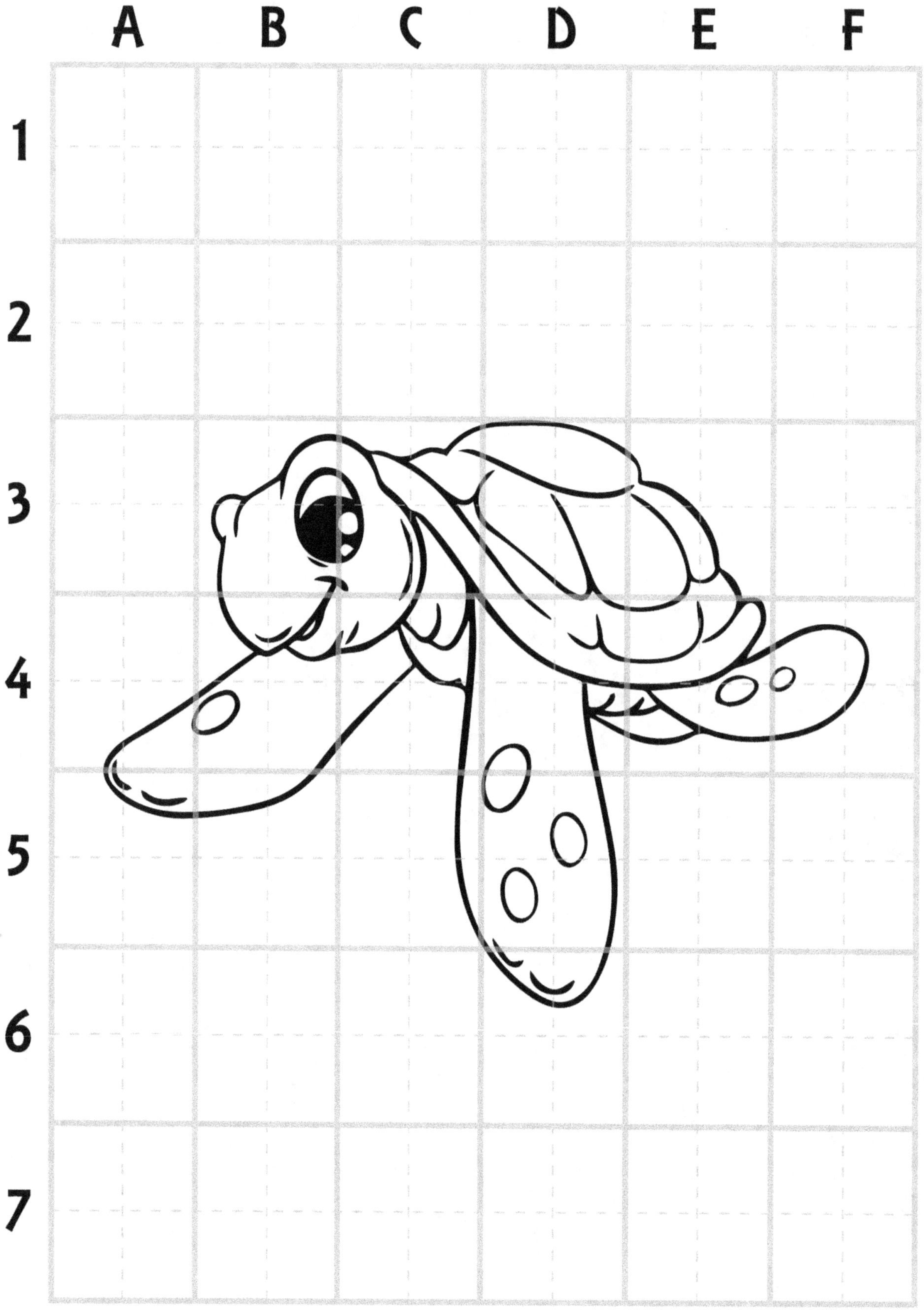

YOUR TURN!

	A	B	C	D	E	F
1						
2						
3						
4						
5						
6						
7						

CAT

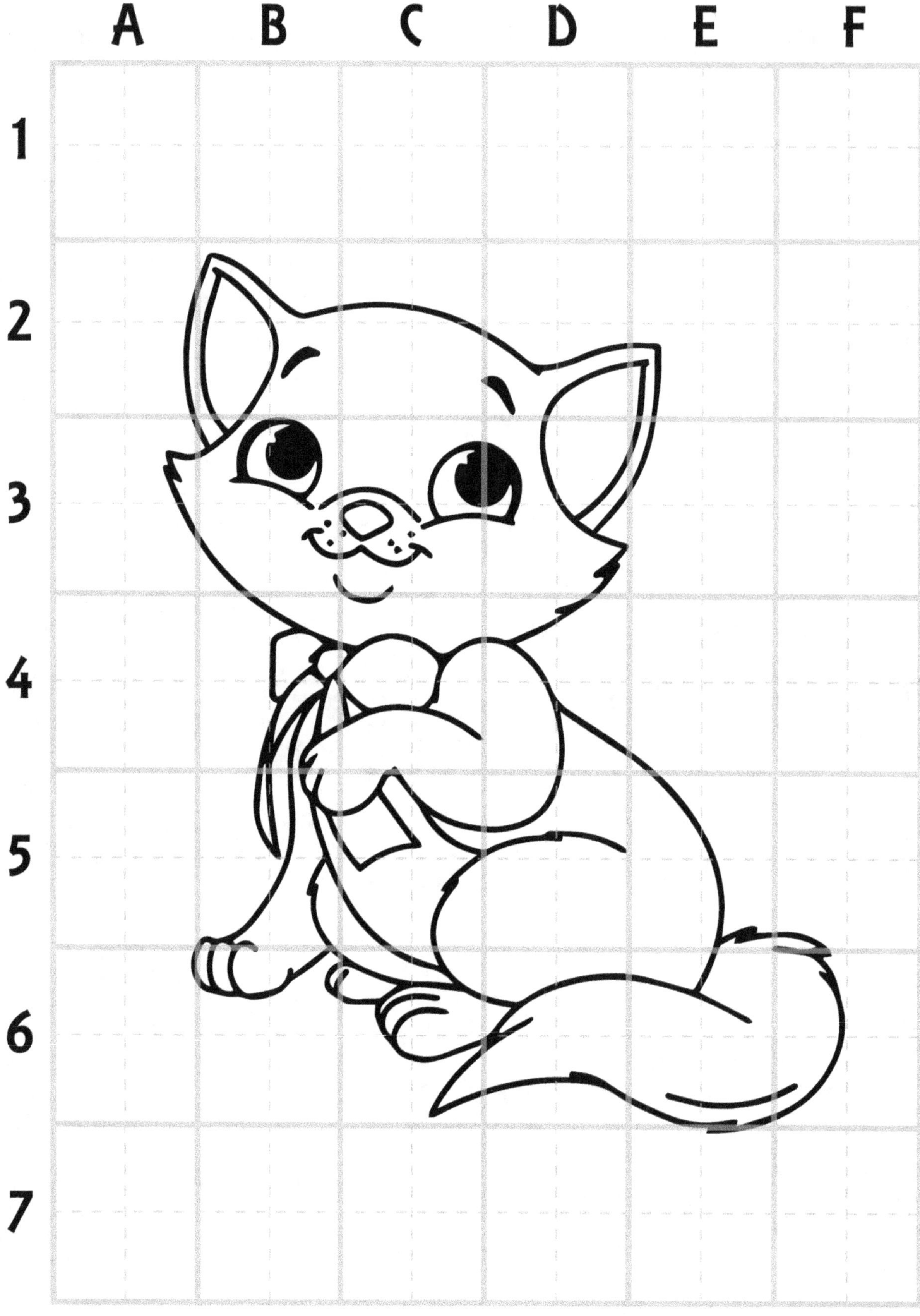

YOUR TURN!

	A	B	C	D	E	F
1						
2						
3						
4						
5						
6						
7						

ELEPHANT

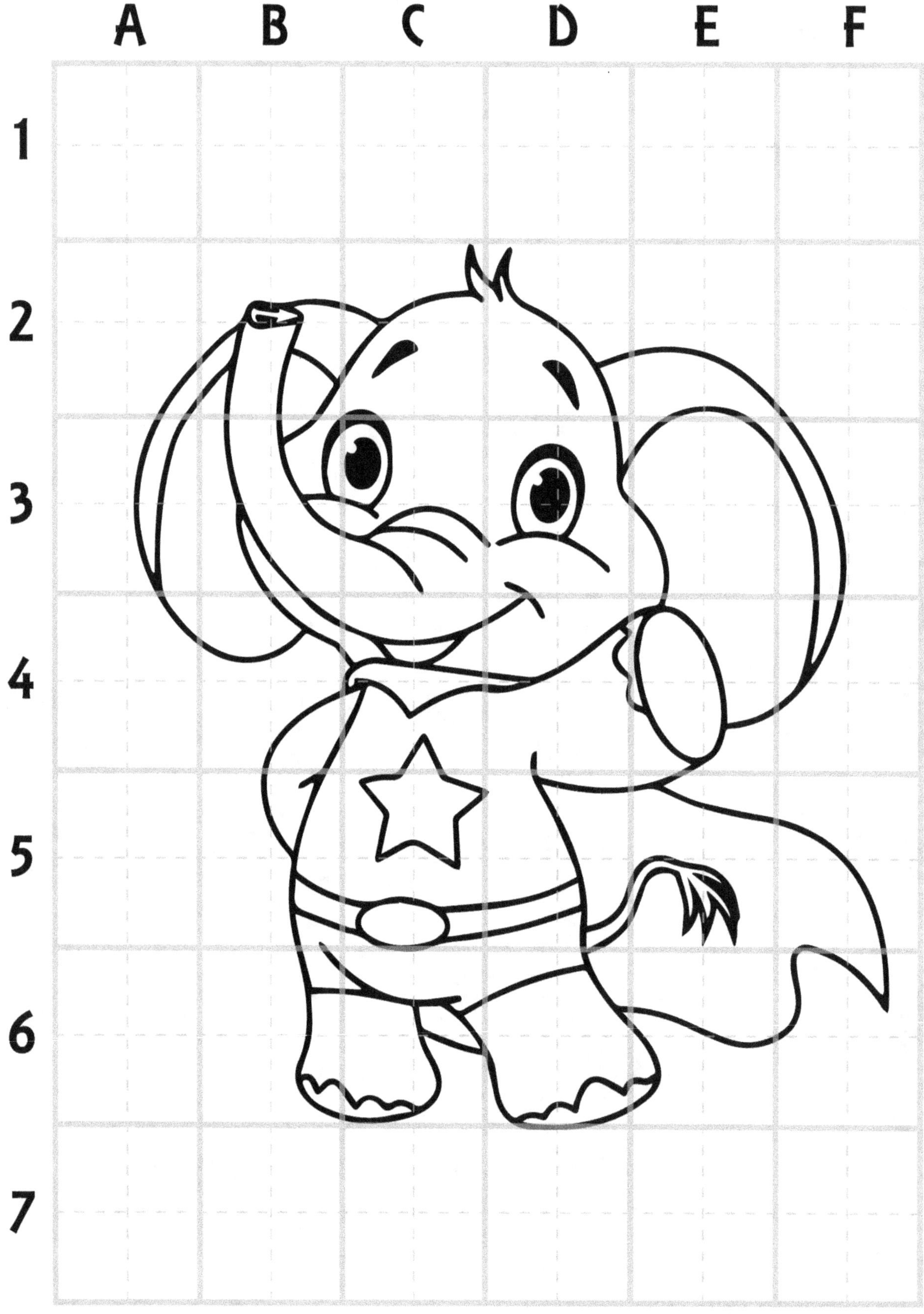

YOUR TURN!

	A	B	C	D	E	F
1						
2						
3						
4						
5						
6						
7						

DOG

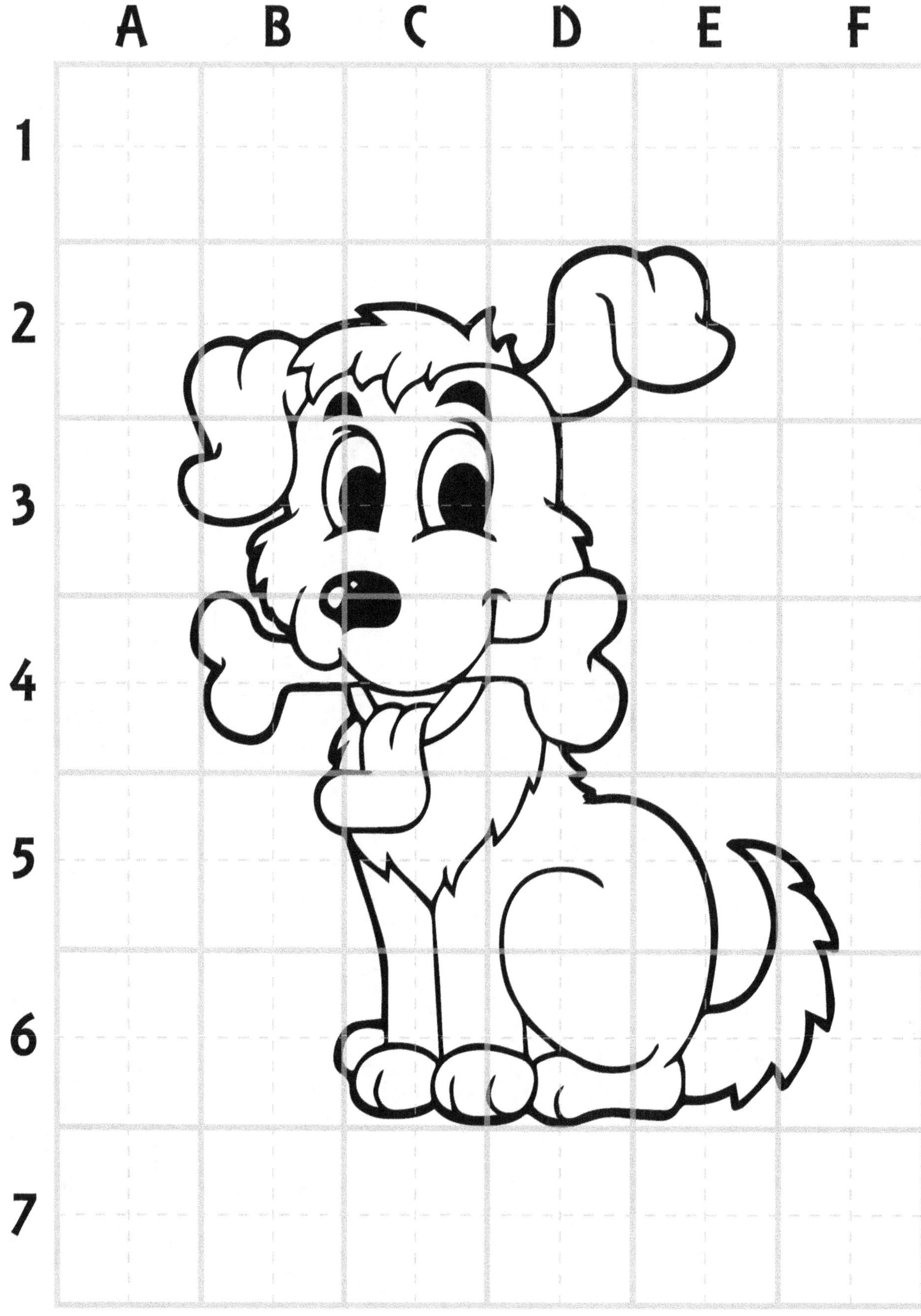

YOUR TURN!

	A	B	C	D	E	F
1						
2						
3						
4						
5						
6						
7						

GIRAFFE

A B C D E F

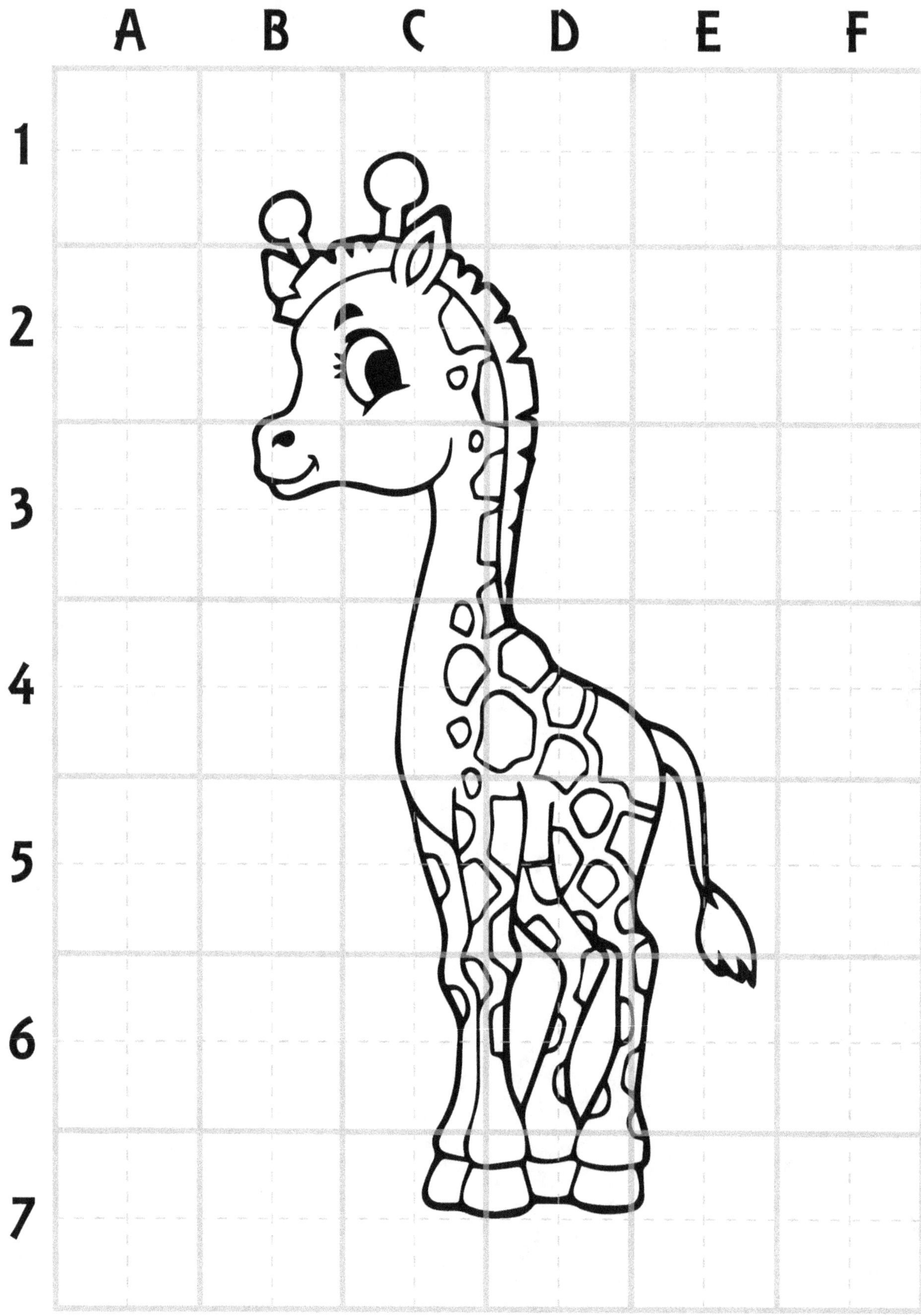

YOUR TURN!

	A	B	C	D	E	F
1						
2						
3						
4						
5						
6						
7						

BIRD

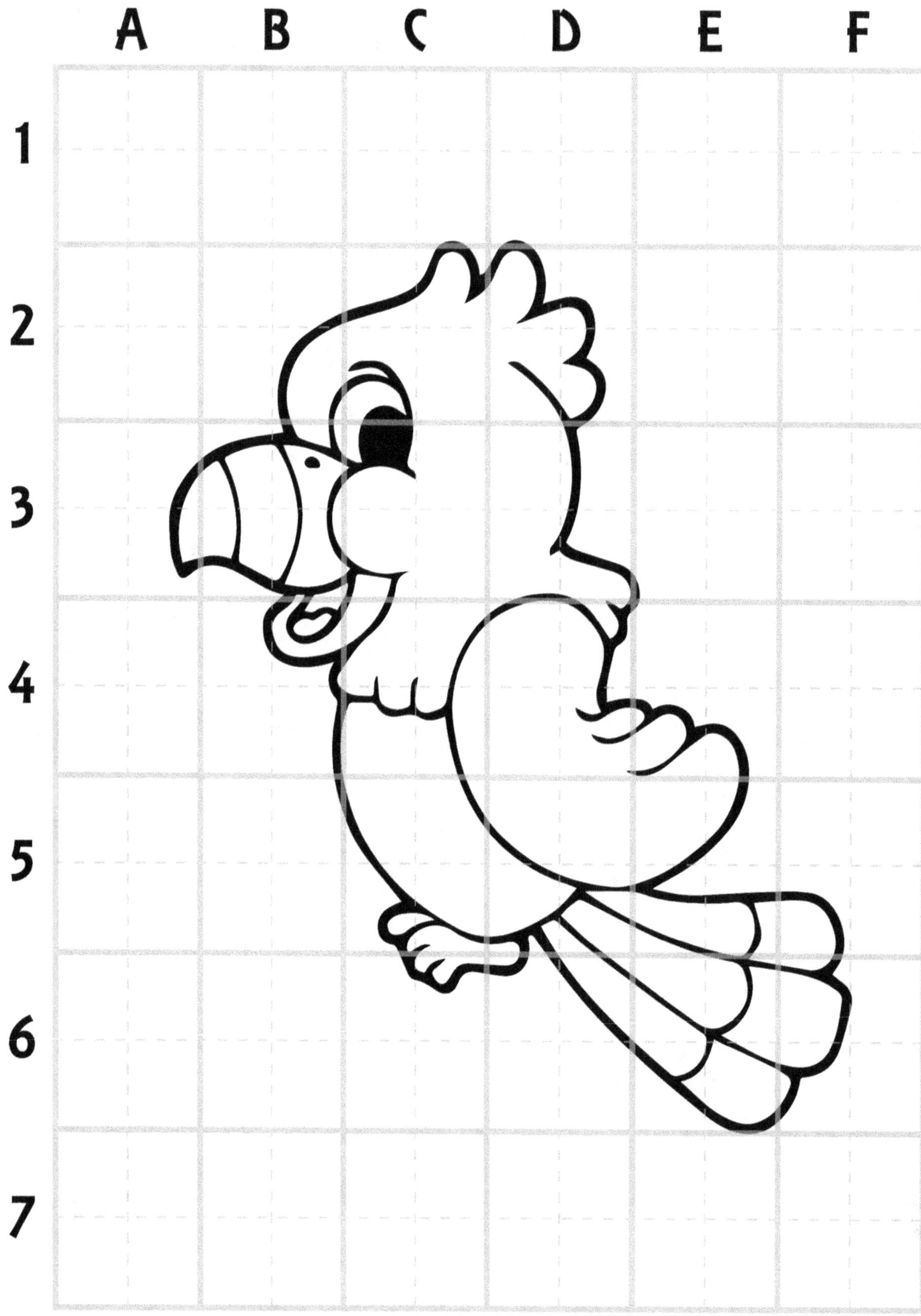

YOUR TURN!

	A	B	C	D	E	F
1						
2						
3						
4						
5						
6						
7						

CROCODILES

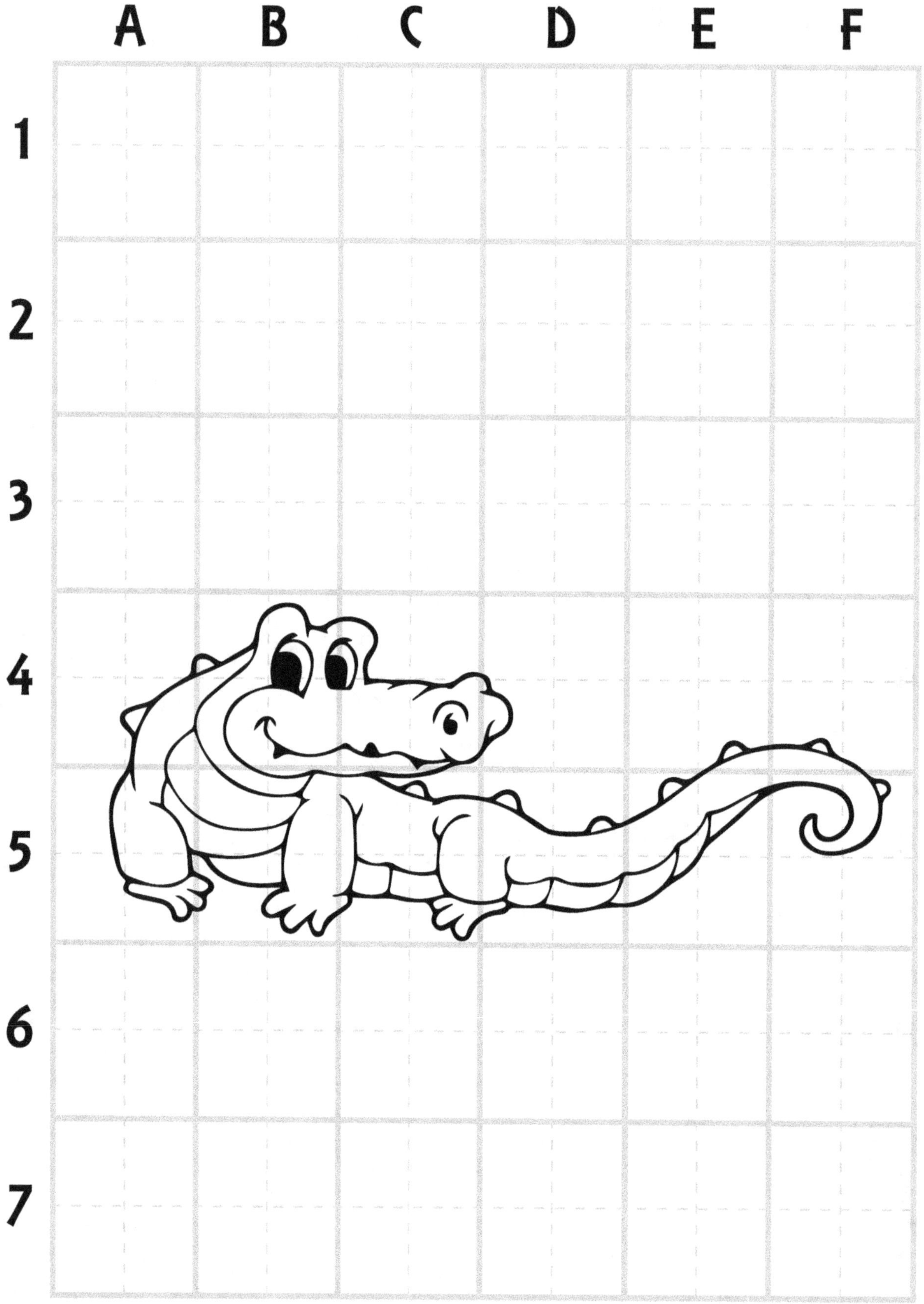

A   B   C   D   E   F

1

2

3

4

5

6

7

YOUR TURN!

	A	B	C	D	E	F
1						
2						
3						
4						
5						
6						
7						

HEN

A B C D E F

1

2

3

4

5

6

7

YOUR TURN!

	A	B	C	D	E	F
1						
2						
3						
4						
5						
6						
7						

KINGFISHER

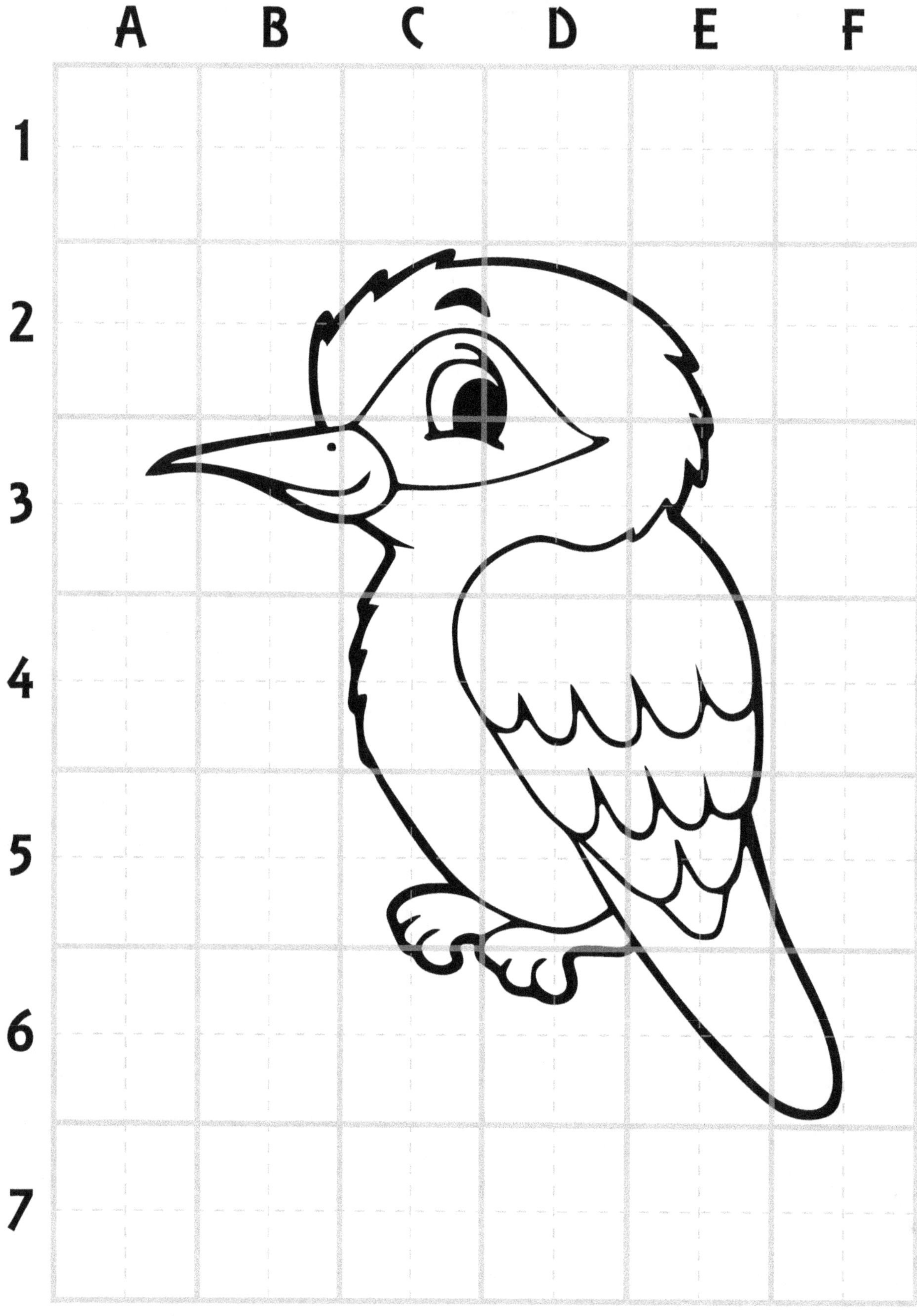

YOUR TURN!

	A	B	C	D	E	F
1						
2						
3						
4						
5						
6						
7						

FISH

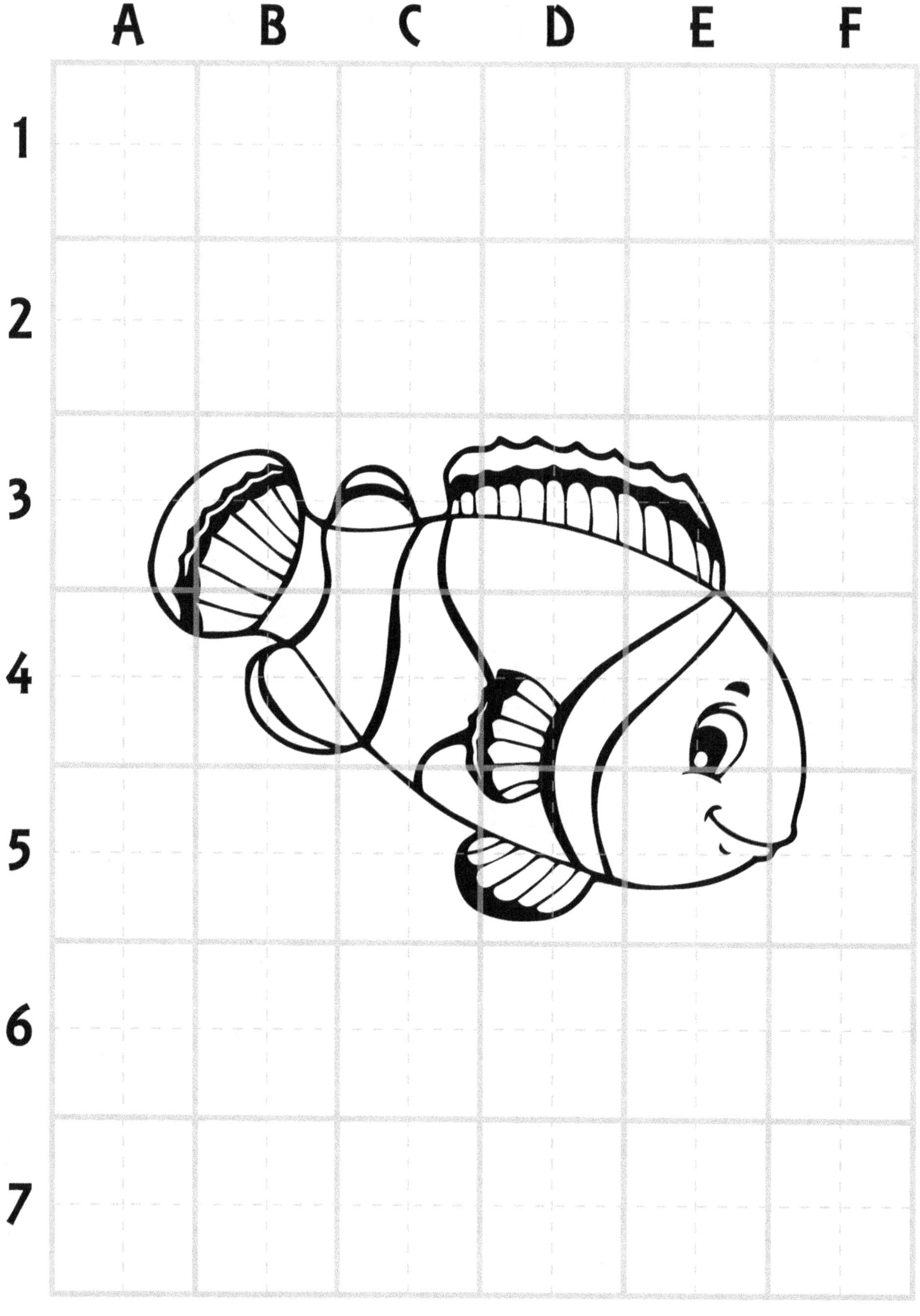

A B C D E F

YOUR TURN!

	A	B	C	D	E	F
1						
2						
3						
4						
5						
6						
7						

SEAHORSE

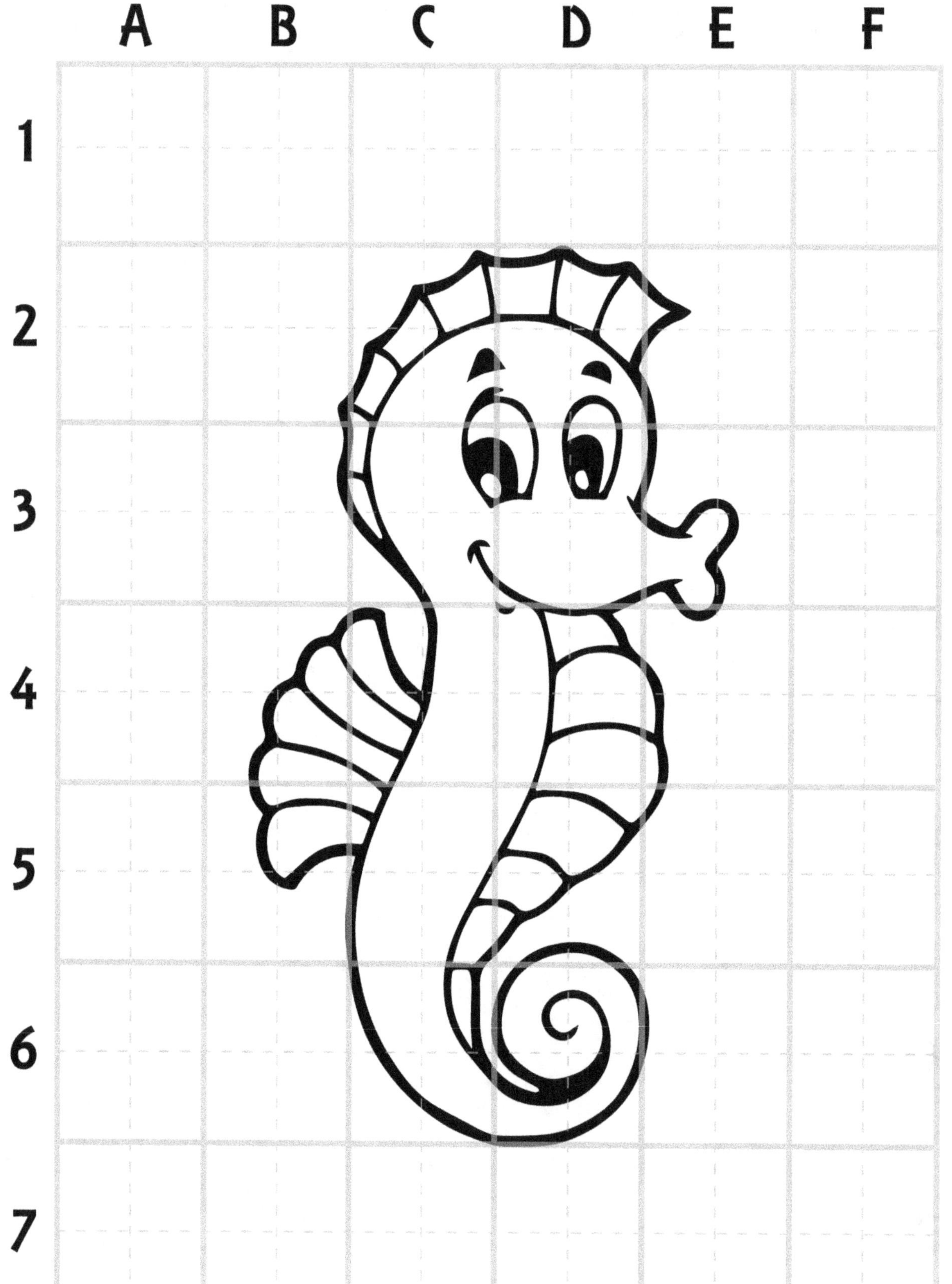

	A	B	C	D	E	F
1						
2						
3						
4						
5						
6						
7						

YOUR TURN!

	A	B	C	D	E	F
1						
2						
3						
4						
5						
6						
7						

DOG

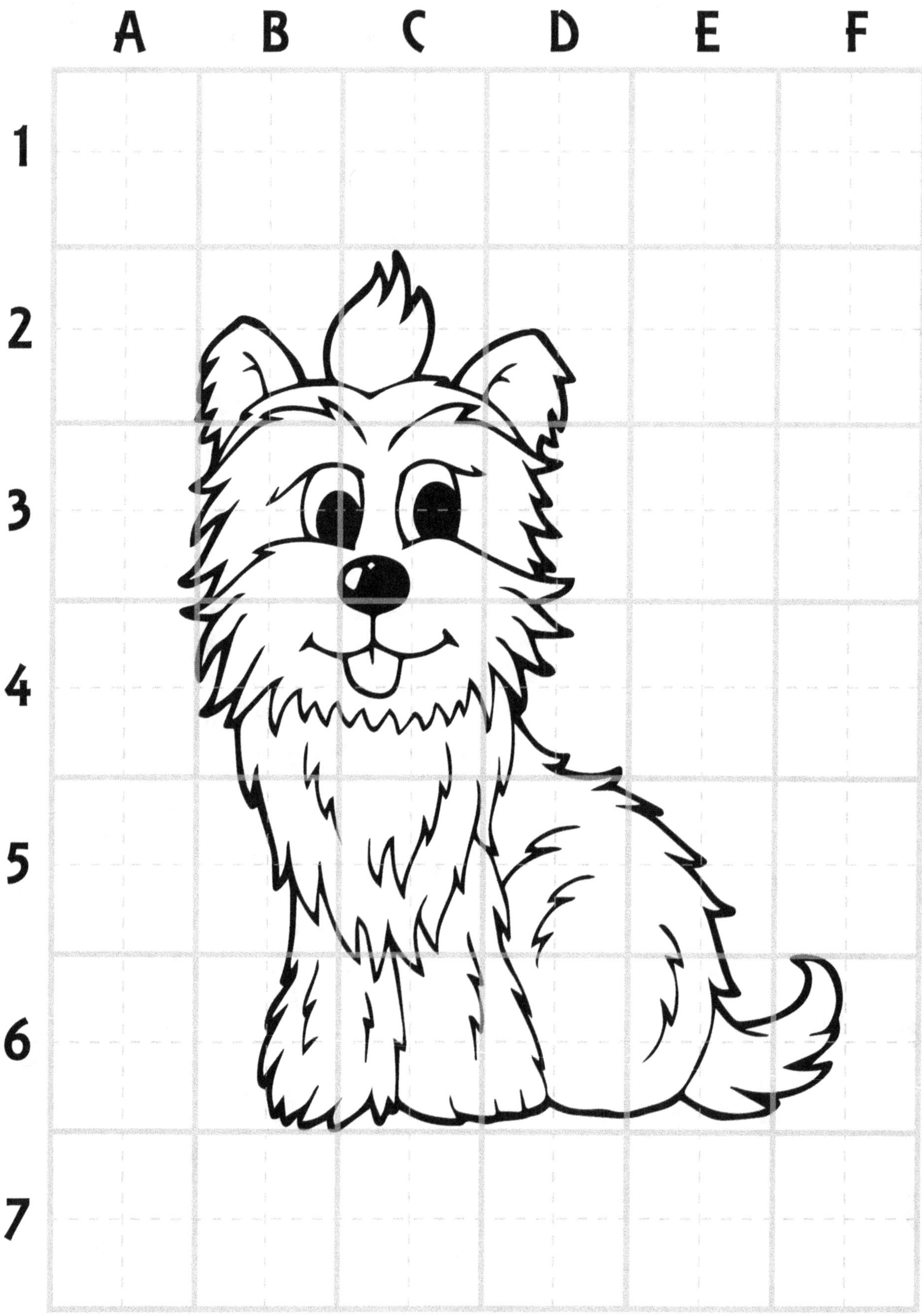

YOUR TURN!

	A	B	C	D	E	F
1						
2						
3						
4						
5						
6						
7						

DOLPHIN

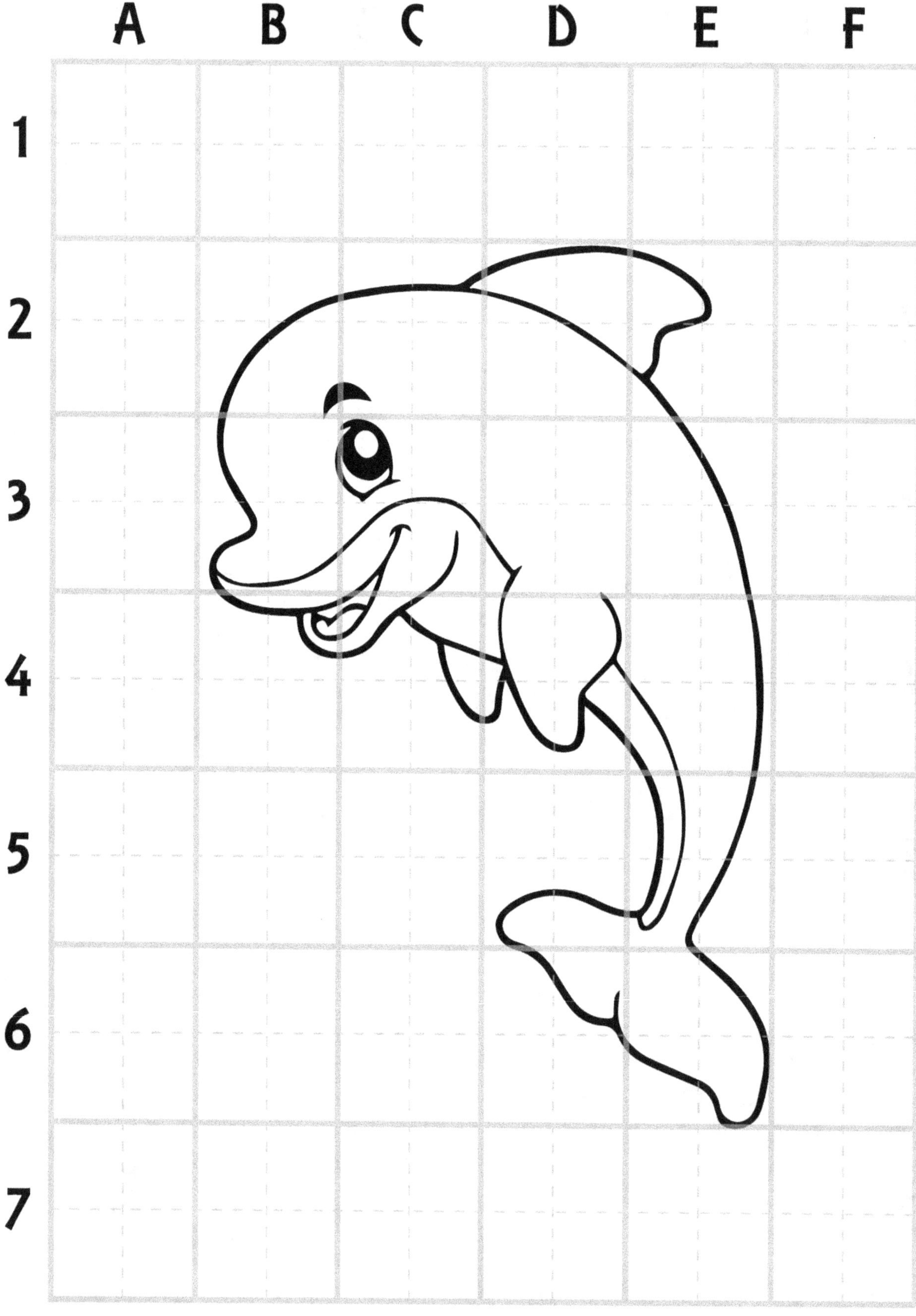

YOUR TURN!

	A	B	C	D	E	F
1						
2						
3						
4						
5						
6						
7						

CRAB

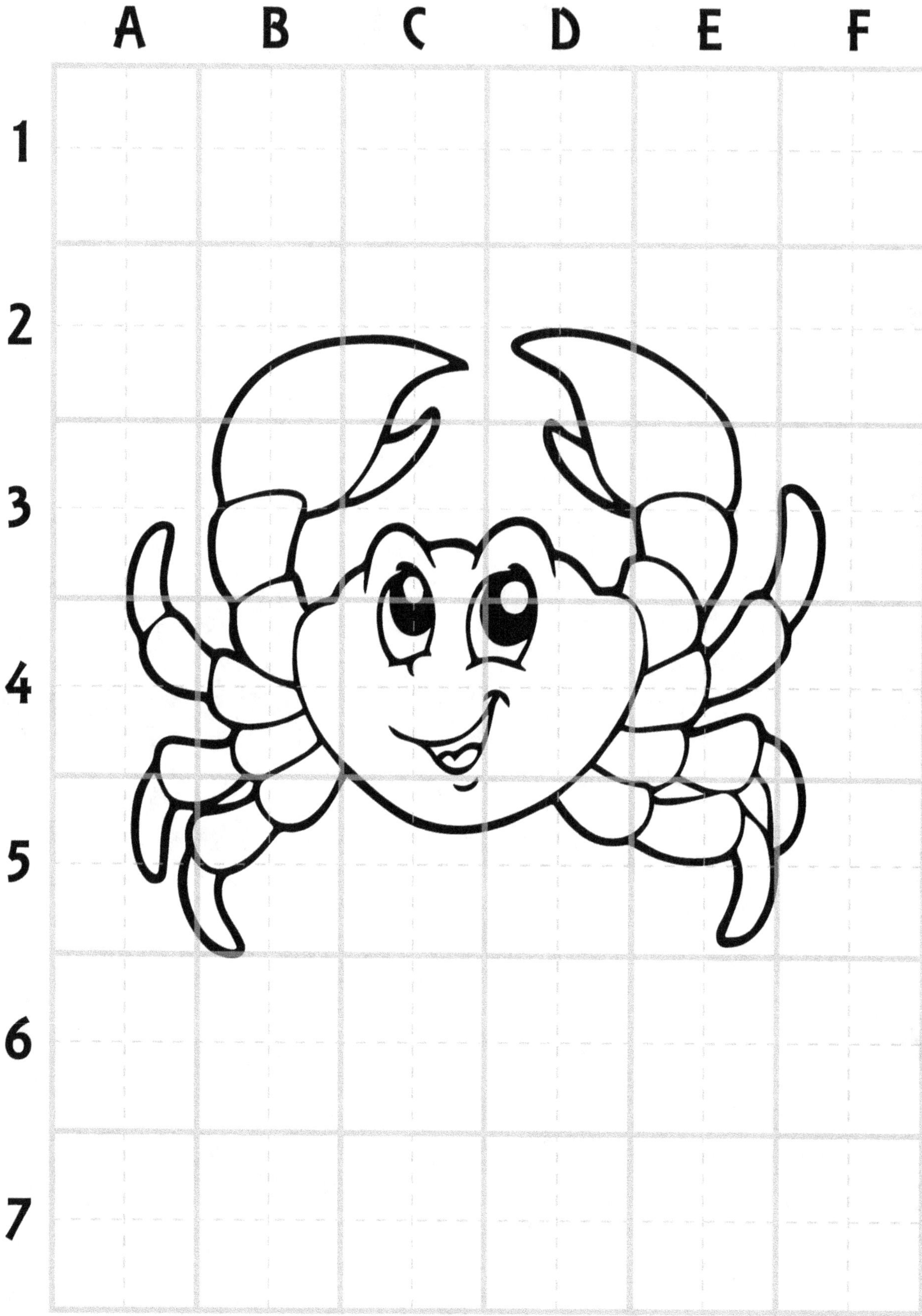

YOUR TURN!

	A	B	C	D	E	F
1						
2						
3						
4						
5						
6						
7						

GORILLA

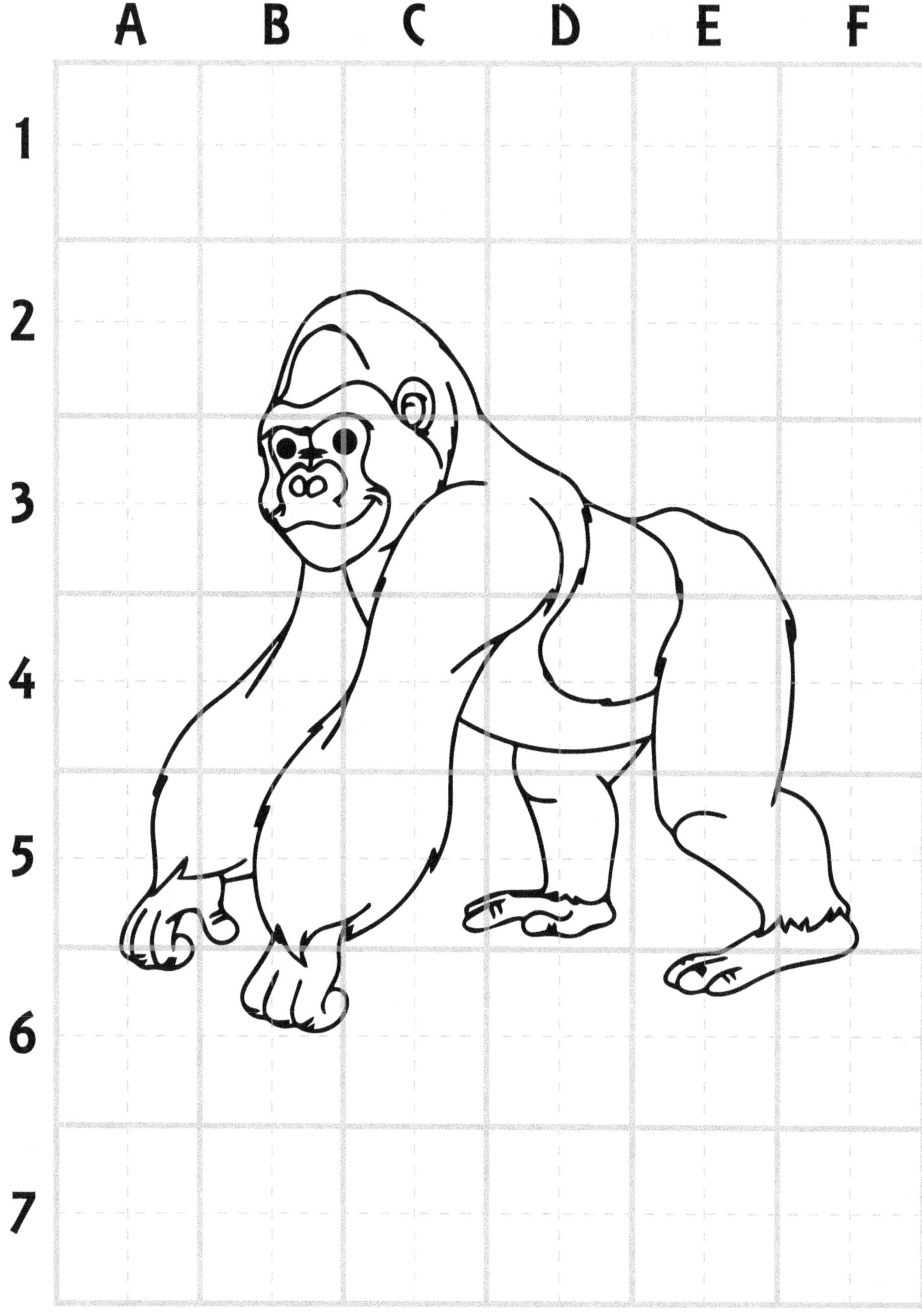

YOUR TURN!

	A	B	C	D	E	F
1						
2						
3						
4						
5						
6						
7						

YOUR TURN!

	A	B	C	D	E	F
1						
2						
3						
4						
5						
6						
7						

YOUR TURN!

	A	B	C	D	E	F
1						
2						
3						
4						
5						
6						
7						

YOUR TURN!

	A	B	C	D	E	F
1						
2						
3						
4						
5						
6						
7						

YOUR TURN!

	A	B	C	D	E	F
1						
2						
3						
4						
5						
6						
7						

YOUR TURN!

	A	B	C	D	E	F
1						
2						
3						
4						
5						
6						
7						

YOUR TURN!

A   B   C   D   E   F

1

2

3

4

5

6

7

YOUR TURN!

	A	B	C	D	E	F
1						
2						
3						
4						
5						
6						
7						

www.ingramcontent.com/pod-product-compliance
Lightning Source LLC
Chambersburg PA
CBHW080519030726
47592CB00012B/3406